NETWORK+

A PRACTITIONER'S STUDY GUIDE

NETWORK+

A PRACTITIONER'S STUDY GUIDE

DAVID LEE EVENDEN
Founder & Owner – StandardUser Cyber Security

JOHN BRETH
Founder & Managing Principal – J. B. Consultants, LLC (J.B.C.)

Oversight: Kent Potter
Book Design: Loryn O'Donnell
Illustrations: Erin DeGroot
Content Contributors: Information Security Practitioners

ISBN-13: 978-1-7344107-0-9

FOREWORD

I'm one of the lucky ones. Over twenty years ago I joined the World's Finest Navy, AKA the United States Navy, and had to learn system administration and internetworking on the fly.

I consider myself lucky because learning how the Internet works and how to build networks has allowed me to be successful in a wide ranging technology career. That success has included work on top technical teams at the National Security Agency, Defense Intelligence Agency, and eventually founding my own cybersecurity software company.

My internetworking knowledge base has been critical in building software designed to help protect networks, while understanding how to build more secure networks from the start.

When I started in this field, I had no clue that we'd all be connected by the same technology that I was using to help share and protect our nation's secrets. But here we are.

This will only continue, and I believe that if you are working in technology, internetworking is a bedrock skill that will serve you well in the job market for several more decades.

This book will give you a foundation not only for a certification, but also for enterprise architecture, cybersecurity, software engineering, and more.

The knowledge in this book is worth hundreds of thousands of dollars, if not millions. You deserve it. We live in a knowledge-based economy, so people will pay you for what you know.

What a time to be alive.

The sky is the limit. Buckle up.

Marcus J. Carey

TABLE OF CONTENTS

NETWORKING CONCEPTS

NETWORKING CONCEPTS

Networked computing has enabled incredible advances in both the speed and quantity of global communications over the last 50 years. With uses ranging from planning and implementing global business operations, to being notified when the fridge runs out of milk, networking is a critical part of modern life.

In this section, we'll cover the most widely-used network architecture model available: the OSI model. Common network ports and protocols will also be covered, so that you have a basic understanding of the types of services running over most networks today.

Lastly, we'll discuss high-level network concepts, like network topologies and characteristics associated with both routing and switching. We'll also introduce you to modern wireless standards and cloud services with their various delivery models.

PORTS & PROTOCOLS

A protocol is the agreed upon method of communication that a service uses to function (such as HTTP, SMTP, DNS). A port is a logical descriptor given to represent a service or process and is identified by its port number. Port numbers below 1024 are defined as "well-known" by RFC 3232, while port numbers 1024 and above are used by the upper layers (more about those in Lesson 3) to set up sessions with other hosts. This lesson covers the following protocols and their associated port numbers:

SSH	22
DNS	53
SMTP	25
FTP	20 & 21
SFTP	22
TFTP	69
TELNET	23
DHCP	67 & 68
HTTP	80
HTTPS	443
SNMP	161
RDP	3389
NTP	123
SIP	5060 & 5061
SMB	445
NETBIOS	137-139
POP	110
IMAP	143
LDAP	389
LDAPS	636
H.323	1720

PROTOCOL TYPES

INTERNET CONTROL MESSAGE PROTOCOL (ICMP): A protocol used by network devices to send error messages and operational indicators to other devices.

USER DATAGRAM PROTOCOL (UDP): A connectionless / stateless protocol which sends data without the need for any prior communications, such as a handshake, or predefined path. It also has no way of verifying that the data has been sent correctly, so it is useful for situations in which verification is unnecessary or done by the application.

TRANSMISSION CONTROL PROTOCOL (TCP): A connection oriented transmission protocol which features reliable, ordered, error-checked delivery of data on a network.

INTERNET PROTOCOL (IP): A protocol which uses the IP address in the packet header to deliver data from one host to another, it is essentially the foundation of the Internet.

PORT 22: SSH

SECURE SHELL: A Command Line Interface (CLI) that provides a secure connection via encryption from one host to another over an unsecured network with client-server architecture. SSH uses TCP port 22 by default.

PORT 53: DNS

DOMAIN NAME SERVICE (DNS) SERVER: A server that operates on TCP and UDP port 53. DNS primarily resolves a hostname to its associated IP Address. For instance, resolving www.website.com to 206.123.114.186, so in essence it is the phonebook of the Internet. It uses TCP for zone transfers and UDP for regular DNS lookups.

PORT 25: SMTP

SIMPLE MAIL TRANSFER PROTOCOL: A standardized protocol for transmitting email data over a network. It uses port TCP 25 by default.

PORTS 20 & 21: FTP

FILE TRANSFER PROTOCOL: A protocol and program that allows users to list and manipulate files and directories between a client and a server. The FTP program uses TCP port 20 or 21 by default.

PORT 22: SFTP

SECURE FILE TRANSFER PROTOCOL: Implements the FTP program over an SSH session. This allows for secure file transferring between devices. SFTP uses TCP port 22 by default because it is built on SSH.

PORT 69: TFTP

TRIVIAL FILE TRANSFER PROTOCOL: A stripped down version of FTP, this increases efficiency at the cost of functionality. For instance, TFTP does not support directory browsing and does not require authentication. TFTP operates on UDP port 69.

PORT 23: TELNET

TELNET: A simple text-based protocol that is primarily used for terminal emulation. It allows a client machine to access the resources of a server machine. Because Telnet is insecure, SSH is the recommended and preferred protocol for accessing server machine resources. Telnet uses TCP port 23 by default.

PORTS 67 & 68: DHCP

DYNAMIC HOST CONFIGURATION PROTOCOL: A protocol that assigns IP addresses to hosts with information provided by a server. It uses UDP port 67 or 68.

PORT 80: HTTP

HYPERTEXT TRANSFER PROTOCOL: A protocol used to manage communication between web browsers and web servers. HTTP operates on TCP port 80.

PORT 443: HTTPS

HYPERTEXT TRANSFER PROTOCOL SECURE: The secure counterpart to HTTP. HTTPS encrypts data transactions between a web browser and server using protocols such as Secure Socket Layer (SSL) and, more commonly, Transport Layer Security (TLS). HTTPS uses TCP port 443 by default.

PORT 161: SNMP

SIMPLE NETWORK MANAGEMENT PROTOCOL: A protocol that collects data about the devices on its network and creates a report at set intervals. It is used to determine the status of a network and notify administrators of issues. SNMP uses port 161 by default.

NOTE: SNMP versions 1 and 2 only support UDP, whereas SNMPv3 adds support for TCP.

PORT 3389: RDP

REMOTE DESKTOP PROTOCOL: A proprietary protocol created by Microsoft that allows a machine to connect remotely to another. While similar in function to Telnet, RDP differentiates itself by using a *Graphical User Interface (GUI)* instead of a command-line interface. RDP uses port TCP 3389 by default.

PORT 123: NTP

NETWORK TIME PROTOCOL: A protocol that ensures that all devices on a network agree on the time. This is very important to ensuring accurate timestamps. NTP uses UDP port 123 by default.

PORTS 5060 & 5061: SIP

SESSION INITIATION PROTOCOL: A protocol used to control sessions in multimedia applications, such as phone calls, video calls or instant messaging. It uses either TCP or UDP port 5060 or 5061 by default.

PORT 445: SMB

SERVER MESSAGE BLOCK: A protocol used for sharing access to files and printers as well as other communications between hosts on a Microsoft Windows network. SMB uses TCP port 445 by default.

> *NOTE:* SMB can run on UDP port 137 & 138, and TCP port 137 and 139 using NetBIOS.

PORTS 137-139: NETBIOS

NETWORK BASIC INPUT / OUTPUT SYSTEM: An Application Program Interface (API) that works only in the upper layers of the OSI model (more on this in Lesson 3). It allows applications on separate computers to communicate over a network. NetBIOS uses TCP and UDP ports 137-139.

PORT 110: POP

POST OFFICE PROTOCOL: A protocol for storing incoming mail (like mail sent using SMTP). When a client connects, POP releases stored mail to the client. The client can then manage the data, rather than the server. The latest version of POP is POP3 which is unencrypted and uses TCP port 110 by default.

> *NOTE:* POP3 is slowly being replaced by IMAP.

PORT 143: IMAP

INTERNET MESSAGE ACCESS PROTOCOL: A protocol for storing incoming mail (like mail sent using SMTP). While similar to POP, IMAP supports additional security and options for handling mail downloads. The current version of IMAP, IMAPv4, supports hierarchically stored data and a search function. IMAP is unencrypted and uses TCP port 143 by default.

PORT 389: LDAP

LIGHTWEIGHT DIRECTORY ACCESS PROTOCOL: A protocol used to access and maintain distributed directory information and is used in concert with Microsoft Active Directory for centralized authentication, or as a standalone centralized authentication method. It allows the sharing of users, systems, services, and applications throughout the network. LDAP operates on TCP and UDP port 389 by default.

PORT 636: LDAPS

LIGHTWEIGHT DIRECTORY ACCESS PROTOCOL SECURE: Uses SSL to secure data transmissions of LDAP. It uses TCP and UDP port 636 by default.

PORT 1720: H.323

H.323: A protocol that provides a standard for video on an IP network. It defines how real-time audio, video, and data information is transmitted and uses the *Real-time Transport Protocol (RTP)* standard. It uses TCP port 1720 by default.

OSI LAYER

This section covers the Open Systems Interconnection (OSI) model, an architectural model that provides a standard for vendors to create networks that are compatible with one another. The OSI model describes how data and network information is communicated from an application on one computer through the network media to an application on another computer.

The OSI model is a hierarchical model of seven distinct layers. The following figures show the seven OSI layers along with their functions.

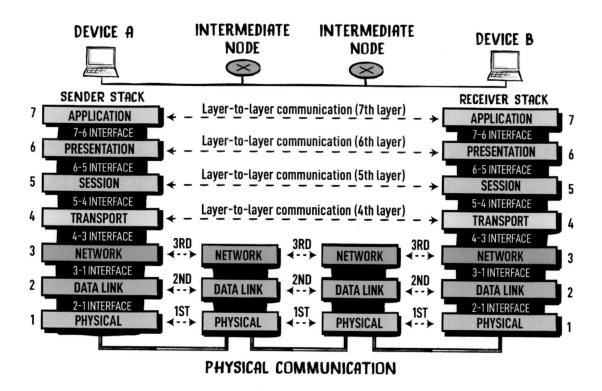

THE UPPER LAYERS

The Upper Layers define the rules of how the applications working within the host machines communicate with each other as well as with end users.

Application (Layer 7)	File, print, message, database, application services, and provides a user interface
Presentation (Layer 6)	Present data, data encryption, compression, and translation services
Session (Layer 5)	Dialog control, keep different applications' data separate

THE BOTTOM LAYERS

The Bottom Layers define how the actual data is transmitted from end to end.

Transport (Layer 4)	End-to-end connection, error correction before resending
Network (Layer 3)	Routing, logical addressing
Data Link (Layer 2)	Framing, combines packets into bytes and bytes into frames, provides access to media using MAC address, error detection (not correction)
Physical (Layer 1)	Physical topology, moves bits between devices, specifies voltage, wire speed, and pin-out of cables

LAYER 7: THE APPLICATION LAYER

The Application Layer is where user programs communicate or interact with the network. This layer determines the availability of communicating partners as well as the resources required to connect them. The Application Layer comes into play only when access to the network will be needed soon, such as when an HTTP request needs to be made.

LAYER 6: THE PRESENTATION LAYER

The purpose of the Presentation Layer is to translate data, format code, and present the data to the Application Layer. This layer will take a native format, such as EBCDIC, and convert it into something generic, such as ASCII. This increases compatibility over a network by ensuring that data transmitted by the Application Layer of one computer is understood by the Application Layer of another computer. OSI standards define how data should be formatted. The Presentation Layer is also responsible for compression, decompression, encryption, and decryption.

LAYER 5: THE SESSION LAYER

The Session Layer is responsible for setting up, managing, and tearing down sessions between Presentation Layer entities. It also provides dialog control between devices or nodes. It coordinates communication between systems and serves to organize their communication by offering three different modes: *simplex*, *half duplex*, and *full duplex*. The Session Layer essentially keeps one application's data separate from another application's data.

LAYER 4: THE TRANSPORT LAYER

The Transport Layer segments and reassembles data into a data stream. It handles the data from upper-layer applications and unites them onto the same data stream, providing end-to-end data transport services. This establishes a logical connection between a sending host and destination host on an internetwork. It is responsible for providing the mechanisms for *multiplexing* upper-layer applications, establishing virtual connections, and tearing down virtual circuits. It also hides many low-level details of network-dependent information from the higher OSI layers. The most prominent protocols are TCP and UDP, and data that is sent at this layer is sent in datagrams.

LAYER 3: THE NETWORK LAYER

The Network Layer manages logical device addressing, tracks the location of devices on the network, and determines the best way to move data. The Network Layer transports data between devices that are not locally attached on the same network. There are two types of *packets* used at the Network Layer:

DATA PACKETS: These are used to transport a user's data through the internetwork. *Routed protocols* are protocols used to support data traffic, i.e., Internet Protocol (IP) and Internet Protocol version 6 (IPv6)

ROUTE UPDATE PACKETS: These are used to update neighboring routers about the networks connected to all routers within the internetwork. They use *routing protocols*, i.e., Routing Information Protocol (RIP), RIPv2, Enhanced Interior Gateway Routing Protocol (EIGRP), and Open Shortest Path First (OSPF). These packets help build and maintain routing tables on each router.

You should also be familiar with the following terms:

NETWORK ADDRESSES: Protocol-specific node addresses. Routers must maintain separate routing tables for each routed protocol to account for multiple addressing schemes (like IP, IPv6).

INTERFACE: This is where a packet will exit when sent to a destination. Interface may refer to the physical port or software interface that data is sent through.

METRIC: This is the distance to the remote network. A variety of methods exist for computing metric, and each routing protocol uses a specific metric. For example, RIP uses a *hop count*--the number of routers a packet passes through en route to a remote network.

NOTES ABOUT ROUTERS:

- Routers break up broadcast domains (meaning less traffic on the network). They also break up collision domains, but this can be accomplished by Layer 2 (Data Link layer) switches as well. By default, routers won't forward any broadcast or multicast packets.
- Routers use the logical address in a Network Layer header to determine the next-hop router to forward the packet to.
- Routers can use *access lists* to control the types of packets that are allowed to enter or exit an interface (for security).
- Routers can provide Layer 2 bridging functions if needed and can simultaneously route through the same interface.
- Layer 3 devices (like routers) provide connections between virtual LANs (VLANs).
- Routers can provide quality of service (QoS) for specific types of network traffic.

LAYER 2: THE DATA LINK LAYER

The Data Link Layer provides the physical transmission of the data and handles error notification, network topology, and flow control. It ensures that messages are delivered to the proper device on a LAN using the MAC address and translates pieces of data, called *data frames*, from the Network Layer into bits for the Physical layer to transmit. When a message is sent between routers, the packets are framed with control information at the Data Link Layer, which is then stripped off by the receiving router. This process is repeated for each hop until the packet reaches its destination. The Data Link Layer has two sublayers:

MEDIA ACCESS CONTROL: MAC defines how packets are placed on the media. Physical addressing and logical topologies are defined here.

LOGICAL LINK CONTROL: LLC is responsible for identifying Network Layer protocols and then encapsulating them. An LLC header tells the Data Link Layer what to do with a packet once a frame is received.

LAYER 1: THE PHYSICAL LAYER

The Physical Layer sends and receives bits (1s and 0s). It communicates directly with the communication media (cables), which may transmit data in different ways (i.e., *state transitions*-- changes in voltage) and require a variety of protocols. The Physical Layer defines the electrical, mechanical, procedural, and functional requirements for activating, maintaining, and deactivating the physical link between end systems.

Lastly, this layer specifies the layout of the transmission media, or topology. A *physical topology* is the way the cabling is physically laid out, whereas a *logical topology* is the signal path through a physical topology.

IP ADDRESS COMPONENT CONFIGURATION

An IP address is a logical address that identifies a machine on a network. It allows a host on one network to communicate with a host on a different network regardless of the type of LANs the hosts are participating in. Below are some important terms in understanding Internet Protocol (IP):

BIT

A binary digit, either a 1 or 0.

BYTE

A byte is 8 bits but 7 or 8 bits can be usable, depending on whether or not parity is used. Most of the time you can assume 8 usable bits.

OCTET

An Octet is always an 8-bit binary number. They are often displayed in decimal up to the value 255.

NETWORK ADDRESS

The designation used to send packets to a remote network or host, i.e., 10.0.0.0, 172.16.0.0, or 192.168.1.10.

IP ADDRESS

A logical address used to define a single host. *IP* will often be used to refer to IPv4, whereas IPv6 will always be written as IPv6.

BROADCAST ADDRESS

This is used by applications and hosts to send information to all hosts on a network. Examples include 255.255.255.255 which designates all networks and hosts, 172.16.255.255 which denotes all subnets and hosts on the network 172.16.x.x.

IP ADDRESSING SCHEME

An IP address is made up of 32 bits of information (4 sections of 8 bits) known as a structured or hierarchical address, i.e. 192.168.1.102. IP addresses will normally be depicted in decimal, but can sometimes be shown in binary (11000000.10101000.00000001.1100110), or hexadecimal (B0.A8.01.BB). IPv6 for example always uses hexadecimal, which will be covered later.

To increase efficiency in finding machines, IP addresses are broken into a two- or three-layer hierarchical addressing scheme, where the first section(s) of an address represent the network, and the last section(s) represent the host. All hosts on a given network have the same network address. This increases efficiency, because a machine can be found faster by narrowing it down to its network. The sections that denote the network and the host are decided by its class:

CLASS A: The first octet represents the network and the last 3 octets represent the host (network.host.host.host). So in the IP address 49.22.102.270, the 49 is the *network address* and 22.102.70 is the host address. Every machine on this network starts with 49.

> *NOTE:* The first bit of the network address must always by 0, giving an address range of 0-127 for Class A addresses.

CLASS B: The first 2 sections are the network address and the latter 2 are the host address (network.network.host.host).

> *NOTE:* The first two bits must be 10, leaving 14 positions left for manipulating in Class B addresses.

CLASS C: The first 3 sections represent the network address, whereas the last section represents the host address (network.network.network.host).

> *NOTE:* The first three bits must be 110 of a Class C address.

CLASS D & E: Addresses that start with 224 or 255 are reserved for Class D and E networks. Class D is used for multicast address and Class E for scientific purposes.

Some addresses are reserved for special purposes, for example:

127.0.0.1	This is the *loopback address*. It allows a host to send packets to itself without creating network traffic.
Host address of all 0s	Interpreted as the *network address*, referring to any host on a specified network. 192.0.0.0 refers to any host on the 192 network.
Host address of all 1s	Refers to any host on a specified network. For example, 126.255.255.255 means "all hosts" on network 126.
0.0.0.0	Means "any network."
255.255.255.255	Broadcast to all hosts on the current network.

PRIVATE VS PUBLIC IP ADDRESSING

Private IP addresses are addresses that are seen only by the private network. They can be resolved on a private network, but they are not routable through the Internet. This adds some security to the network and also saves a lot of address space. To translate the private IP address for use on the Internet, a Network Address Translation (NAT) is used. This is a very common practice that most all organizations use, as almost all organizations use private IP space on their internal networks. Some common examples of private IP addresses are 192.168.0.0/24, 10.0.0.0/8, and 172.16.0.0/16.

A Public IP Address, on the other hand, is routable through the internet and is visible to any host you connect to.

DEFAULT GATEWAY

A gateway is a node that serves as an access point to outside networks. The *default gateway* is the gateway that nodes on the network default to when attempting to access outside resources. In a home or small office, this would be the router, which connects the local network to the Internet.

VIRTUAL IP

A Virtual IP Address is an address that does not map to an actual network interface. They are often advertised by NAT devices, which then route any traffic the address receives to an actual IP address.

SUBNET MASK

Subnetting is taking a network address, and breaking it up to create smaller *subnetworks*. The benefits of this include reducing network traffic, optimizing network performance, simplifying management, and facilitating the span over large geographical distances.

To define a subnet, you take bits from the host portion of the IP address and reserve them to define the subnet address (much like a network address). For this to work properly, all hosts must know which part of the address will be used as the subnet address. This is done by assigning a *subnet mask* to each machine. The subnet mask is a 32-bit value that allows the recipient of the packets to distinguish the network ID portion of the IP address from the host ID portion. The 1s in the subnet mask indicate the part of the address that is the subnet address.

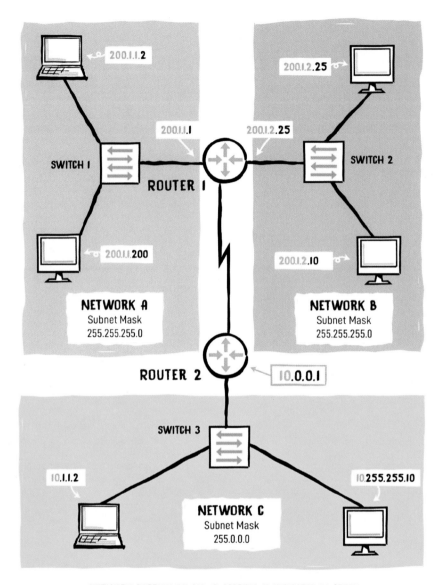

NETWORK PORTION OF ALL IP ADDRESS IS INDICATED IN GREEN.
IP ADDRESS AT ROUTER INTERFACE IS DEFAULT GATEWAY.

NETWORK	NETWORK ADDRESS	BROADCAST ADDRESS
A	200.1.1.0	200.1.1.255
B	200.1.2.0	200.1.2.255
C	10.0.0.0	10.200.255.255

VARIABLE LENGTH SUBNET MASK: VLSM refers to the ability to divide an IP address space into a hierarchy of subnet masks. These subnets can be of different sizes and contain a different number of hosts. This is important because it allows for many hosts to be created without wasting a lot of address space.

CLASSLESS INTER-DOMAIN ROUTING: CIDR is an important term to know. It is a method of allocating a number of addresses to a network. When your network is allocated a block of addresses (like from an Internet Service Provider), it will look something like: 192.168.10.32/28. The number after the slash tells you how many bits are turned on in the subnet mask. Below are some subnet masks with their respective CIDR values.

BEYOND NETWORK+
For a tutorial and more in depth information on subnetting, check out **https://www.subnetting .net/Tutorial.aspx**

SUBNET MASK	CIDR VALUE
255.0.0.0	/8
255.128.0.0	/9
255.255.0.0	/16
255.255.255.0	/24
255.255.255.252	/30

NOTE: A Class A address has a minimum of 255.0.0.0, Class B has a minimum of 255.255.0.0, and Class C has a minimum of 255.255.255.0. The maximum is 255.255.255.252 for an IPv4 address. It's important to note that IPv6 addresses can go up to /64.

ADDRESS ASSIGNMENTS

When a machine is connected to a network, it needs a way of obtaining a valid IP address. This can be done through some of the following methods:

DYNAMIC HOST CONFIGURATION PROTOCOL: DHCP server that assigns IP addresses to hosts automatically on a network. A network administrator assigns a pool of addresses to the DHCP server to be assigned. Any host on the network will request IP information such as an IP address and the address of other servers on the network. The DHCP server then leases that information to the host for a set amount of time.

DHCPV6: This works similar to DHCP, with the addition of support for IPv6 addresses.

STATIC: A static IP address can either be assigned manually or be assigned by the DHCP server if configured to do so. A static IP does not change like one normally leased from a DHCP server.

STATELESS AUTOCONFIGURATION (EUI-64): This solution allows a device to address itself by first looking at the network address from the router and then appending its own MAC address as the interface ID. For IPv6, the missing 16 bits are padded in the middle with FFFE. For example, the MAC address 0050:d673:1987 would become 0260:d6FF:FE73:1987 (where 0260 is the network address).

AUTOMATIC PRIVATE IP ADDRESSING: APIPA is a method provided by Windows that allows a host to assign itself the minimum required information to allow it to communicate when a DHCP server isn't available. Think of it like a DHCP failover.

IP RESERVATION: Certain IP addresses can be reserved in a DHCP configuration to prevent it from being assigned to a random machine. This is useful if you want DHCP to manage an IP address that should remain static.

IPV6 CONCEPTS

Due to the lack of expandable public IPv4 address space as the Internet continued to grow, a plan for a new routed protocol that would take IPV4's place was implemented.
This resulted in the creation of the IPv6 protocol. IPv6 has the following benefits over IPv4:

- Exponentially increased IP space which ensures that NAT is no longer a necessity, 2^32 (4.29 billion) public IPv4 addresses, compared to 2^128 (roughly 340 undecillion, 282 decillion, 366 nonillion, 920 octillion, 938 septillion)
- More efficient routing due to simplified headers and aggregated routing tables
- Built-in mobility and security features
- Optimized fragmentation and improved quality of service (QoS)

BEYOND NETWORK+
For additional information on IPv6 address shortcuts check out **networklessons.com/ipv6/shortening-ipv6-addresses**

While taking these improvements into account, it is important to understand the following concepts of IPv6 addresses.

ADDRESSING

IPv6 addresses are 128 bits in length, granting them many more addresses than IPv4. IPv6 addresses are broken up into eight groups, rather than four, which are separated by colons. Also, IPv6 uses hexadecimal instead of base 10. This essentially means you have eight groups with 16 bits in each group.

Here is an example of an IPv6 address: 2001:0db8:3c4d:0012:0000:0000:1234:56ab. In this example, the first three sections are the *global prefix*, the fourth group is the subnet, and the last four groups are the *interface ID*. A shorthand notation for IPv6 exists, where each group's leading 0's is removed. In this case, the address above would look like 2001:db8:3c4d:12::1234:56ab.

DUAL STACKING

Dual stacking is a process that allows your network to use both IPv4 and IPv6, making it the easiest and most common method of migrating from IPv4 and IPv6. A dual-stack router is able to support both IPv4 and IPv6 packets, allowing you to upgrade your network devices one at a time.

TUNNELING

6to4 tunneling is the process of creating a tunnel for IPv6 information to travel through a regular IPv4 network. It works by having a dual-stack router identify any IPv6 packets traveling along the network and apply an IPv4 header to them. This header is then removed by a dual-stack router on the other end of the tunnel and the packet is passed to the destination using IPv6.

NEIGHBOR DISCOVERY

Rather than using ARP and broadcasts to discover what devices are on a network, IPv6 has an improved method called *neighbor discovery*. Neighbor discovery uses ICMPv6 and multicast to discover other devices on the network. There are five messages involved in the process:

ROUTER SOLICITATION: When a device first joins a network, it will try to find the router by sending this type of message. Because multicast is used, only routers will get this message.

ROUTER ADVERTISEMENT: After receiving a Router Solicitation, the router will send a Router Advertisement directly to the sending host. The Router Advertisement will suggest to the host how it can obtain an IPv6 address (either from a DHCP server or through dynamic allocation).

> *NOTE:* The router will also send out Router Advertisements periodically to all hosts on its network.

NEIGHBOR SOLICITATION: A Neighbor Solicitation message replaces ARP on an IPv6 network. This message is sent to a neighboring host to receive its IPv6 address or verify the cached address is still valid.

NEIGHBOR ADVERTISEMENT: A Neighbor Advertisement is sent in response to a Neighbor Solicitation. It contains the IPv6 address of the sending host.

REDIRECT: This is a message used by routers to indicate the best route a host can use to send a message. When a router receives a packet, it will either forward that packet to its destination, or respond with a Redirect message to tell the host there is a better route.

DISTRIBUTED SWITCHING

Distributed switching is an architecture in which switches are placed at strategic places throughout a network. A common use is in a network that spans multiple buildings. A switch can exist in each building that connects to the devices in that building. Each building then connects to a main switch to create an internetwork.

PACKET-SWITCHED VS CIRCUIT-SWITCHED NETWORKS

In a packet-switched network data is moved based on the destination address in each packet. When the packet is received, they are reassembled in the proper sequence to create the message.

Circuit-switched networks require dedicated point-to-point connections to transmit data. These types of networks are used primarily for phone calls while packet-switched networks are used for data.

SOFTWARE-DEFINED NETWORKING

Software-defined Networking (SDN) is an architecture in which network control is entirely programmable and that control is separated from the physical devices that are actually providing the routing. SDNs are designed to be more flexible and configurable than traditional hardware-based networks.

ROUTING

Routing is the process of moving packets from one network to another network using routers. It's important to make the distinction between a routed protocol and a routing protocol. A *routing protocol* is a tool used to find all networks in an internetwork and make sure they have the same routing table, i.e., RIP, RIPv2, EIGRP and OSPF. A *routed protocol* is used to send packets through the established internetwork. There are three main types of *routing protocols*.

DISTANCE-VECTOR ROUTING PROTOCOLS

ROUTING INFORMATION PROTOCOL: RIP is one of the oldest distance-vector routing protocols, it uses a hop-count as a routing METRIC. To prevent loops, it caps the hop-count at 15, which also limits the size of network it can support.

ENHANCED INTERIOR GATEWAY ROUTING PROTOCOL: EIGRP is a protocol created by Cisco, and unlike RIP, it uses incremental updates to reduce the amount of data to be transmitted.

LINK-STATE ROUTING PROTOCOLS

OPEN SHORTEST PATH FIRST: OSFP is a protocol using the Shortest Path First (SPF) algorithm (also known as Dijkstra's Algorithm) to find the shortest path to a node through the network.

HYBRID

BORDER GATEWAY PROTOCOL: BGP is a protocol that makes decisions based on paths, network policies, or rule-sets configured by a network administrator to determine routes.

DISTANCE-VECTOR & LINK-STATE ROUTING PROTOCOLS: Generally used on internal networks, whereas BGP is the primary routing protocol used on the Internet.

GET FAMILIAR WITH THESE ROUTING TYPES:

STATIC: Static routing does not change. They have to be entered manually into a routing table.

DYNAMIC: Enables neighboring routers to share routing information with each other and update their routing tables.

DEFAULT: Default routing is used when no path is specified for a packet. In this event, the router sends the packet to the *default route*.

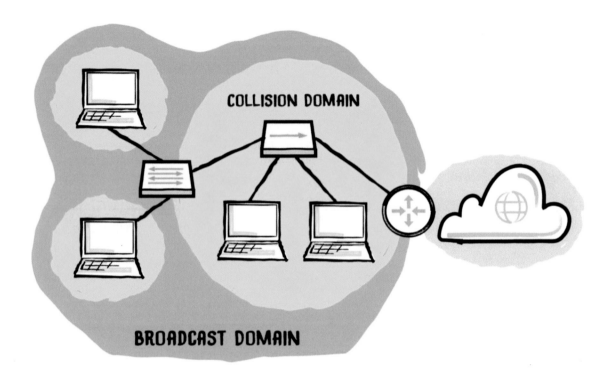

BROADCAST DOMAINS: A broadcast domain is a section of a network in which hosts can communicate via a broadcast. Any hosts that are connected by a hub or switch and are in the same subnet are in the same broadcast domain.

CSMA/CD: Carrier-Sense Multiple Access with Collision Detection (CSMA/CD) is a method of communicating data in which carrier-sensing is used to defer transmission until no other nodes are transmitting. This prevents collisions from occurring.

CSMA/CA: Carrier-Sense Multiple Access with Collision Avoidance (CSMA/CA), like CSMA/CD, is a method of communicating data in which carrier-sensing is used, but nodes attempt to avoid collision by only transmitting when the medium is sensed to be idle.

COLLISION DOMAINS: A collision domain is a segment of a network where data collisions may occur. A data collision occurs when two nodes try to transmit data simultaneously on the same medium. Each physical port off of a networking device (bridge, switch, router, firewall, etc.) is its own collision domain.

PDU: A Protocol Data Unit is a piece of information that is sent as a single unit through a network. This may refer to a bit, a frame, or a packet.

MTU: A Maximum Transmission Unit is the size of the largest PDU that can be transmitted in an OSI Layer 3 transaction.

BROADCAST: A broadcast is a message sent by a node on a network which is received by all other nodes on that broadcast domain.

UNICAST: A unicast message is sent from one node to only one other node.

MULTICAST: A multicast message is a message sent by a node that is addressed to multiple other nodes. Only the nodes to which the message is addressed will receive the message.

PERFORMANCE CONCEPTS

TRAFFIC SHAPING: Traffic shaping is a process in which certain types of packets are delayed or dropped to improve the performance for other packets.

QUALITY OF SERVICE: QoS is the ability of a network to prioritize types of traffic based on of configurable tags and provide varying levels of quality service depending on the configured importance of the traffic. This means low latency, reduced jitters, and dedicated bandwidth.

DIFFERENTIATED SERVICE: DiffServ is a network architecture that creates a scalable mechanism for providing QoS.

CLASS OF SERVICE: CoS is a parameter in many data communication protocols that identifies the type of payload a packet contains. This is useful for giving priority to certain packets.

NAT/PAT

Network Address Translation (NAT) enables hosts on separate networks to communicate by translating IP addresses of one network to match the network address of the other network. A common example of this is requesting a webpage. When requesting a webpage, you use the public IP address of the web server you are accessing. However, when your router receives this request, it translates your IP address to its own public IP address. It does this because the web server would not be able to send a response directly back to your private IP address, so the router acts as a middle man.

For your router to keep track of which devices on the network it should send responses to, it keeps a *translation table* that maps the requested resource with the private IP that requested it. Port Address Translation works similarly to NAT, however it uses different ports to differentiate the requesting hosts to overcome the address limitations of a one-to-one NAT.

PORT FORWARDING

Port forwarding is a process performed by your router that forwards traffic on a certain port to a specific host on the network. For example, you might have a web server, with a private IP address of 192.168.1.100, running on port 80 in your network. Hosts outside of your network cannot access your website using your private IP address, so to enable access you will configure your router, with a public IP address of 255.65.101.20, to forward all traffic on port 80 to your web server. Now any host can access your website using 255.65.101.20:80.

ACCESS CONTROL LISTS

An ACL specifies access control entries (ACEs) which allow or deny access to services. ACLs are able to filter based on port numbers, IP addresses, content, or other attributes. ACLs are the first line of defense in controlling which devices can communicate with other devices within and between networks.

SWITCHING

A switch is a hardware device that forwards data received to a destination. It operates similar to a hub, with the added functionality of only forwarding traffic to the segment with the destination MAC address. The main purpose of a switch is to break up a *collision domain*. Switches create private, dedicated collision domains per physical interface and provide independent bandwidth on each port, unlike hubs. Switches operate at Layer 2, which means they can only forward traffic between hosts on the same network/subnet. In order for traffic to communicate between different networks/subnets, a switch must forward that traffic to a Layer 3 device, such as a router.

BRIDGING VS SWITCHING

Switches are almost like bridges with extra ports, but there are some important differences as well as similarities to take note of:
- Bridges are software based, whereas switches are hardware based because they use Application-Specific Integrated Circuits (ASIC) chips to help make filtering decisions.
- A switch can be viewed as a multiport bridge.
- There can be only one *spanning-tree* instance per bridge, whereas switches can have many.
- Switches normally have more ports than bridges.
- Both forward Layer 2 broadcasts.
- Both learn MAC addresses by examining the source address of each frame received.
- Both make forwarding decisions based on Layer 2 addresses.

It's also important to know the following functionalities provided by Layer 2 switching devices:

ADDRESS LEARNING: Layer 2 switches and bridges keep track of the MAC addresses they receive frames from and store them in the *forward/filter table*. Initially, the switch floods each port with data until it receives a frame back, at which point it can associate that MAC address with a port.

FORWARD/FILTER DECISIONS: If the destination hardware address is known by the switch when it receives a frame, it makes a *forward/filter decision* and only sends the frame to the specified exit interface. This prevents wasted bandwidth in other segments; this is called *frame filtering*.

LOOP AVOIDANCE: Loop avoidance is very important to preventing *thrashing* and dropped frames. It's solved with the Spanning Tree Protocol (STP).

SPANNING TREE PROTOCOL: STP's main task is to prevent network loops, which it does by constantly monitoring the network, examining the links, and shutting down any redundant ones. There are 5 distinct states that a bridge or switch running STP can be in:

- **BLOCKING:** A blocked port will drop all frames except Bridge Protocol Data Units (BPDUs) to prevent using loops.

- **LISTENING:** The port listens to BPDUs to make sure no loops occur before passing data frames. A port in this state prepares to forward data frames without populating the MAC address table.

- **LEARNING:** This state is where the port listens to BPDUs and learns all the paths in the switched network.

- **FORWARDING:** The port sends / receives all data frames on the bridged port. If the port is still a designated or root port at the end of the learning state, it enters forwarding state.

- **DISABLED:** A port in this state does not do anything. An administrator must set this state.

NOTE: Bridges / switches break up collision domains. Routers break up broadcast domains.

VIRTUAL LANS (VLANS)

A VLAN is a logical grouping of a network's users and resources connected to administratively defined ports on a switch. VLANs are often associated with a unique network/subnet. When creating a VLAN, you create smaller broadcast domains within a Layer 2 switched internetwork by assigning the various ports on the switch to different subnetworks. Frames broadcasted onto the network are only switched between the ports logically grouped within the same VLAN. You would still need a router to create communication between interconnected VLANs (i.e. a layer 3 device must be used to route packets between separate networks/subnets). Each VLAN is assigned a uniquely numbered tag. VLANs are broken up into two different number ranges; the standard range is 1-1005 and the extended range is 1006-4094.

TRUNKING (802.1Q)

Trunking is a technology that enables networks to provide access to many VLANs over the same physical connection. A trunk is a point-to-point link between two switches, a switch and router, or even a switch and server. With this system, you can make a single port part of multiple VLANs at the same time with subinterfaces (this allows you to create multiple logical interfaces that are hosted on one physical interface). When two VLANs exist on the same port, each frame must be tagged to identify which VLAN it belongs to, this is called *Frame Tagging*. IEEE 802.1q was created by IEEE as a standard method of frame tagging. It works by inserting a field into the frame to identify the VLAN.

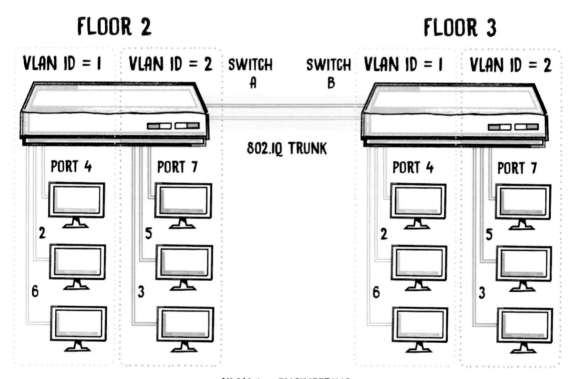

PORT MIRRORING

Port Mirroring is the process of sending copies of network packets seen on one switch port or VLAN to another port. This is commonly used for monitoring traffic.

POE AND POE+ (802.3AF, 802.3AT)

POWER OVER ETHERNET: POE technology sends current and data over ethernet to power devices such as cameras or wireless access points (WAP). The original version is denoted by 802.3af and provides 15.4 W of DC power. Version 802.3at (PoE+) provides up to 25.5 W.

DEMILITARIZED ZONE

A DMZ adds an additional layer of security to a network by restricting what an outside network can see and communicate with on an organization's internal network. It does this by creating a unique security zone that all externally sourced traffic must traverse through. Often times various types of scanning or proxy devices are put into a DMZ, so that external traffic never communicates directly with internal resources. A company would put all of their externally facing services in a DMZ, to limit external exposure of their internal network.

NETWORK TOPOLOGIES

A network of devices (whether wired or wireless) must be configured in some kind of organized structure to meet its operational objectives. This pattern is called a *network topology*. A physical topology is the actual way network devices are connected together via cables and physical interconnections, whereas a logical topology is how the traffic actually moves throughout the network. Whether wired or wireless, it is important to be familiar with these common topologies.

STAR TOPOLOGY

A Star Topology is a network in which all of the nodes are connected to a central node, such as a hub, switch, or wireless access point. A chief benefit of star topology is that if one node goes out, the other nodes can continue to work because they are all connected individually to the central node.

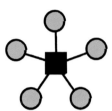

RING TOPOLOGY

In a Ring Topology each node is connected to the next with the last node connecting back to the first to create a ring. This topology isn't very efficient because to add a node you must disconnect an existing node. This brings down the entire network. Additionally, ring topology is expensive, difficult to configure, and not fault-tolerant.

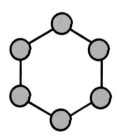

MESH TOPOLOGY

Mesh Topologies are the most convoluted of networks. Each node in the network is connected to each other node, this creates a lot of physical connections. This topology is uncommon in the industry except for a few *hybrid mesh networks* used in Wide Area Networks (WANs) which have many connections for redundancy, but are not full mesh networks. The Internet is an example of this.

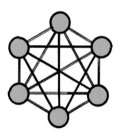

BUS TOPOLOGY

A Bus Topology is one of the most basic types. It consists of a main line (or bus) that all of the nodes are connected to. To add a node you would commonly have to add a "T" to the line and connect an Ethernet cable to the T to create a new node. As it is connected by a single cable backbone, this is a single point of failure and is not fault-tolerant.

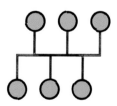

AD HOC TOPOLOGY

An Ad Hoc Topology is a wireless topology where the setup is based on the needs of the specific network. Each node participates by forwarding data to other nodes, this is really only practical for a wireless topology.

INFRASTRUCTURE TOPOLOGY

An Infrastructure Topology is used to extend LANs to support wireless devices. They often use WAPs to provide a way to network both wired and wireless devices.

NETWORK TYPES & TECHNOLOGIES

In addition to Network Topologies, it also important to know the different types of networks, as well as network technologies that facilitate things like the Internet of Things (IoT). Below are some of the most important Network Types and Technologies.

TYPES OF COMPUTER NETWORKS

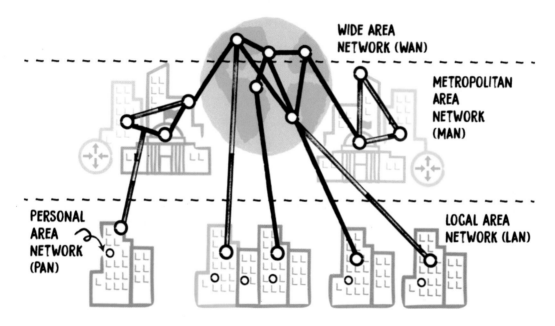

NETWORK TYPES

LOCAL AREA NETWORK: A LAN connects devices within a short range.

WIRELESS LOCAL AREA NETWORK: A WLAN is similar to a LAN with the added functionality of being wireless. WLANs are frequently referred to as Wi-Fi.

WIDE AREA NETWORK: WANs extend over large geographical distances. They are used to relay data to devices in various parts of the world. The Internet can be considered a WAN.

METROPOLITAN AREA NETWORK: A MAN is a network larger than a LAN, but smaller than a WAN. A good example of this is a city-wide network.

CAMPUS AREA NETWORK: Also referred to as a corporate area network, a can is a collection of interconnected LANs normally resides in a limited geographic area. Smaller than MAN and WAN.

STORAGE AREA NETWORK: A SAN is a network that provides access to consolidated storage. They are often used to enhance storage devices so as to make them appear to operating systems as locally attached storage devices.

PERSONAL AREA NETWORK: Used to connect personal devices, PANs can also be connected to another network to uplink to the internet, and are most often used with Bluetooth.

NETWORK TECHNOLOGIES

Z-WAVE: A wireless protocol used mostly for smart homes. It is a mesh network that communicates from appliance to appliance.

ANT+: A protocol developed to collect sensor data, such as a tire gauge or heart monitor.

BLUETOOTH: A standard for exchanging data wirelessly over short distances. It is used frequently to create PANs.

NEAR-FIELD COMMUNICATION: NFC technology allows devices to communicate when placed within 4 cm of each other. They are popularly used for electronic payment systems.

INFRARED RADIATION: IR has a lower frequency than visible light and is almost always invisible to the naked eye. IR is often used for things such as TV remotes.

RADIO-FREQUENCY IDENTIFICATION: RFID uses electromagnetic fields to automatically identify chips which store small amounts of data. They can be used like a barcode, but with the added benefit of not needing to be in sight of the reader.

IEEE 802.11: This is a set of specifications for creating WLANs. They are the world's most widely used networking standards.

WIRELESS TECHNOLOGIES

802.11 STANDARDS

As mentioned before, the *IEEE 802.11* standards are a set of specifications for creating WLANs that are very popular. Below is a list of the different standards under IEEE 802.11 along with what year they were ratified, their frequency, number of non-overlapping channels, transmission type, and data rates. See Appendix for a description of Transmission Types.

	802.11	802.11b	802.11a	802.11g	802.11n	802.11ac
Year Ratified	1997	1999	1999	2003	2010	2013
Frequency Band	2.4 GHz	2.4 GHz	5 GHz	2.4 GHz	2.4 GHz – 5 GHz	5 GHz
# of Channels	3	3	Up to 23	3	Varies	Varies
Transmission Type	IR, FHSS, DSSS	DSSS	OFDM	DSSS or OFDM	DSSS, CCK, OFDM	OFDM
Data Rates (Mbps)	1, 2	1, 2, 5.5, 11	6, 9, 12, 18, 24, 36, 48, 54	1, 2, 5.5, 11 or 6, 9, 12, 5.5, 11	100+	1000+

CELLULAR TECHNOLOGIES

There are three major cellular technologies.

GLOBAL SYSTEM FOR MOBILE COMMUNICATIONS: GSM, as of 2014, is the global standard with over 90% of market shares and operating in over 219 countries and territories. GSM was originally created to replace 1G (an analog solution) with 2G (a digital solution) and has since evolved to include data communication via General Packet Radio Services (GPRS) and EDGE, alternatively via Enhanced Data rates for GSM Evolution (EGPRS).

CODE DIVISION MULTIPLE ACCESS: CDMA is a channel access method used by various radio communication technologies. It offers multiple accesses, where several transmitters can send information simultaneously over a single communication channel. CDMA relies on spread-spectrum technology and a special coding scheme to prevent interference.

TIME DIVISION MULTIPLE ACCESS: TDMA is a channel access method for shared-medium networks. It allows multiple users to share the same frequency by dividing the signal into different time slots.

2.4 GHZ VS 5.0 GHZ

The main difference between a 2.4 and 5.0 GHz network is range and bandwidth. 5.0 GHz provides faster data rates at shorter distance. 2.4 GHz provides farther coverage at slower speeds.

WIRELESS CONFIGURATION

CHANNEL BANDWIDTH

The *Channel Bandwidth* is the frequency range between lowest and highest attainable frequency while meeting a well-defined impairment level in signal power. Increasing bandwidth can increase internet speed, but it can also increase interference.

CHANNEL BONDING

Channel Bonding is an arrangement of communication links where links are combined together either to create redundancy or increase throughput.

MIMO / MU-MIMO

Multiple-Input and Multiple-Output (MIMO) is a method for increasing the capacity of a radio link using multiple transmit and receive antennas. MIMO has become an essential part of wireless communication standards.

Multi-User-MIMO (MU-MIMO) is a set of MIMO technologies in which a set of wireless terminals, each one with multiple antennas, communicate with each other. MU-MIMO adds multiple access support to MIMO.

UNIDIRECTIONAL / OMNIDIRECTIONAL

A *Unidirectional* antenna is one that only allows data to travel in a single direction. It's often used in high-security networks to guarantee information security. Unidirectional antennas often get further range than their omnidirectional counterparts because they focus in a single direction.

An *Omnidirectional* antenna is one that allows data to travel in every direction. This is much more common for wireless networks such as a WAP.

SITE SURVEYS

A *Site Survey* is a survey that gauges the quality of your wireless network and is vital to making sure your wireless network quality is premium or even viable. There are generally three different types of wireless site surveys: passive, active, and predictive. A passive wireless survey involves using tools to detect and measure the strength of the wireless capabilities, but there is no connecting to any of the wireless networks. An active wireless survey involves connecting to a location's wireless networks and measuring the performance on the network. Lastly, a predictive wireless survey utilizes simulation tools to replicate the potential layout and RF characteristics and obstructions of the potential environment.

CLOUD NETWORKING CONCEPTS

TYPES OF SERVICES

SOFTWARE AS A SERVICE: SaaS is a model in which software is licensed on a subscription basis and is centrally hosted. This has become a common service for many companies who use things such as a payroll service or office applications.

PLATFORM AS A SERVICE: PaaS is a category of cloud computing that allows consumers to develop, run, and manage applications without the complexity of building the infrastructure from the ground up. Google Firebase is an example of this.

INFRASTRUCTURE AS A SERVICE: IaaS refers to online services that provide APIs for interfacing with low-level network infrastructure. AWS EC2 is an example of this.

CLOUD DELIVERY MODELS

PRIVATE: This is a solution owned and managed by a company for only the company's use.

PUBLIC: Public Clouds are resources offered by third parties.

HYBRID: Hybrid Clouds allow the use of features from both a private and public cloud.

CONNECTIVITY METHODS

EXISTING INTERNET CONNECTION: When connecting via a browser you will use TLS to securely access resources.

VIRTUAL PRIVATE NETWORK: A VPN requires additional resources such as firewalls/remote servers to securely access resources.

DIRECT CONNECTION: This is the most secure method, by requiring all connections via a private designated connection between the company's network and the cloud provider.

SECURITY POLICIES

CLOUD ACCESS SECURITY BROKER: A CASB sits between users and the cloud in some way to facilitate control. The following are four main characteristics of a CASB:

- VISIBILITY: Being able to see what applications are in use

- COMPLIANCE: Determine if users are complying with protocols

- THREAT PREVENTION: Only allow authorized users to prevent attacks

- DATA SECURITY: Making sure all interactions are encrypted and secured properly.

NETWORK SERVICES

DNS SERVICE

DNS is a foundational protocol on every network and is primarily used to resolve host names to IP addresses. As mentioned before, it is the equivalent of a phonebook for devices connected to a network. You should be familiar with the following DNS properties:

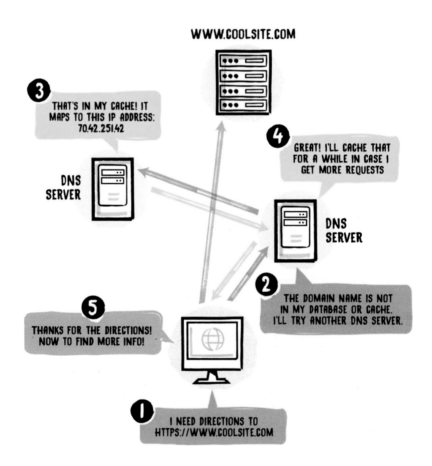

HIERARCHY

DNS operates in a hierarchy with each level separated by a dot. An example is images.google.com, where 'images' is a Third-Level, 'google' is a Second-Level, and 'com' is a Top-Level domain.

INTERNAL, EXTERNAL, AND THIRD PARTY DNS

INTERNAL DNS: Managed completely inside a network and resolves hosts within the network. This is good for networks that have a need to connect to different hosts within the network via a hostname.

EXTERNAL DNS: Allows you to access external DNS information, such as that provided by Google. This is necessary for external access to the Internet via hostnames.

THIRD PARTY DNS: A way of outsourcing internal DNS functionality. It is a cloud based system for managing local records.

RECORD TYPES

A, AAAA: These records simply give you the IP address when given the host name, this is a *Forward Zone*. Note that A is for IP and AAAA is for IPv6.

PTR: This record does the opposite of an A or AAAA record, which is giving a host name when given an IP address. This is a *Reverse Zone*.

MX: Mail Exchange records used to translate mail records. The MX record points to the mail exchanger for a particular host.

CNAME: Canonical Name (CNAME) records are alias records, allowing hosts to effectively have more than one name.

NS: A Name Server record identifies the DNS servers responsible for a zone/domain.

SRV: Service records specifies the hostname and port or a particular service.

TXT: Text records allow arbitrary text to be associated with a host.

SPF: Sender Policy Framework is a security measure for mail records to prevent people from sending emails on your behalf. It specifies an IP address that emails in your name can be sent from.

DKIM: DomainKeys Identified Mail is also a security measure that signs email messages with a key to identify it as yours.

DHCP SERVICE

Dynamic Host Configuration Protocol is an important part of any network. As mentioned in the previous section on IP addresses, this protocol is used to automatically provide IP addresses to devices connected to a network.

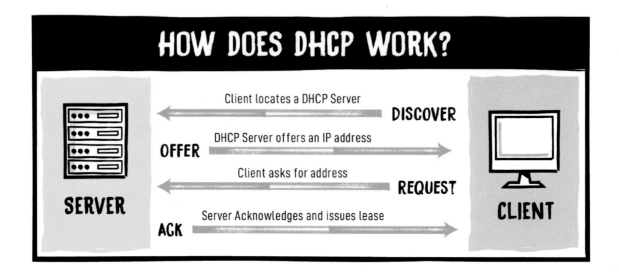

MAC RESERVATIONS: Allows you to reserve an IP address for a specific MAC address

POOLS: A range of IP Addresses used for assigning to specific Subnet Masks or VLANs

IP EXCLUSIONS: Prevent specific IP Addresses from being leased out.

SCOPE OPTIONS: Options including IP Address range, Subnet Mask, Lease Duration, DNS Server, Default Gateway, WINS Server.

LEASE TIME: The amount of time an IP Address is assigned to a specific machine.

- **T1 TIMER:** A timer to indicate when to check in with the DHCP Server to renew the address. This is set to half of the lease time by default.

- **T2 TIMER:** A timer to indicate, if the original DHCP Server is down, when to try renewing with any other DHCP Server. This is set to 7/8ths of the lease time by default.

TIME TO LIVE: TTL is the time it takes for a record to take effect.

DHCP RELAY/IP HELPER: A configuration on a router that converts DHCP broadcasts to unicasts and back in order to allow devices to communicate with the DHCP server that otherwise couldn't.

IP ADDRESS MANAGER: A service that allows you to manage IP addresses, report on usage, control reservations, and manage IPv4 and IPv6.

NETWORK TIME PROTOCOL: NTP is a protocol to make sure time is consistent across devices. This is important for being able to compare time logs.

INFRASTRUCTURE

INFRASTRUCTURE

This section is all about the infrastructure that enables modern networking. Just about every packet on the Internet passes through fiber optic cables buried deep underground or deep on the ocean floor. Many packets are still delivered to the home through decades-old copper phone lines literally hanging in the wind. Almost all packets, Internet or local, fiber or copper, pass through at least one network device to make it to their intended recipient.

We'll first cover hardware cabling and industry standards. Then, network device placement and installation will be introduced so you'll understand how to setup simple, secure, flexible networks.

We'll then move on to introduce more advanced network devices, such as proxies, load balancers, network storage solutions, and intrusion detection systems. Virtual networks will also be covered as they are becoming a logical alternative to physical infrastructure. Finally, you'll learn about Wide-Area Networks (WANs) and the technologies that support them.

CABLING

One of the most important parts of any network is the cabling. The type and quality of cable used determines the effectiveness of the network. This section will explain different cabling concepts.

MEDIA TYPES: The media type refers to the material the cable is made from. The media type can affect the conductivity and therefore the effectiveness of the connection, below are the most common media types.

- COPPER

    - *Unshielded Twisted Pair*: UTP cable is made of individually insulated wires that are twisted together in pairs.

    - *Shielded Twisted Pair*: STP is similar to UTP with an added metal layer around the cable to protect it from interference.

    - *Coaxial*: Contains a center conductor made of copper that's surrounded by a plastic jacket with a braided shield over it. Either PVC or FEP (teflon) is used as the plastic.

- FIBER

    - *Single-mode*: Allows only one light ray through and is used more often for spanning long distances.

    - *Multimode*: Allows multiple light pulses through the fiber and is used more often for short distances.

- PLENUM VS PVC

    - *Polyvinyl chloride*: PVC is cheaper, but can be a fire hazard if used incorrectly.
    - *Fluoroethylene propylene (plenum)*: More expensive, but often required by fire codes, especially when being run inside walls or ceilings.

CONNECTOR TYPES

Equally important to a correctly connected network are the connector types. Below are some of the connectors you will need to be familiar with.

- COPPER

    - *RJ-45* : Registered Jack 45 is a connector for UTP cable, mostly used for Ethernet.

    - *RJ-11* : Registered Jack 11 is also used for UTP cable, but is more commonly used for telephone connections.

    - *BNC* : Bayonet Neill-Concelman connectors are the type most commonly attached to a coaxial cable.

    - *DB-9* : A D-Subminiature 9 connector with 2 rows and a total of 9 pins. It is often used to connect a monitor to a PC.

    - *DB-25* : Similar to a DB-9 but instead has 25 pins.

    - *F-type* : This connector is used with coaxial cable, similarly to BNC. It is popularly used for TV signal or radio.

- FIBER

    - *Local Connector*: LC is a safer style of Small Form Factor (SFF) connector that's becoming more popular.

    - *Straight Tip*: ST connectors are one of the most widely used today, created by AT&T for fiber-optic.

    - *Square Connector*: SC is another very popular fiber-optic connector, which includes a latch to secure it in place. They can come in APC or UPC format.

    - *Ultra-Polished Connectors*: UPC connectors have a straight cut and can sometimes have db loss because some of the signal is reflected back through the cable.

    - *Angle Polished Connectors*: APC is a connector with an angled cut, this increases the performance by reducing the amount reflected back through the cable.

    - *Mechanical Transfer Registered Jack*: MTRJ was the first widely used SFF connector, being only a third of the size of SC and ST.

TRANSCEIVERS

Transceivers are devices that facilitate both transmitting and receiving data. Below are some common types used in networking.

- ### GIGABIT INTERFACE CONVERTER
  GBIC is a standard transceiver often used for gigabit ethernet.

- ### SMALL FORM-FACTOR PLUGGABLE
  SFP is often called mini-GBIC, and performs the same function with a smaller form factor.

- ### SMALL FORM-FACTOR PLUGGABLE PLUS
  Enhanced SFP that supports up to 16 Gbits/s.

- ### QUAD SMALL FORM-FACTOR PLUGGABLE
  QSFP is another small form-factor transceiver that performs the same functions as SFP, but at speeds up to 4 Gbps. The base format is made of four 1 Gbps channels. Other iterations include QSFP+ (40 Gbps) up to QSFP56 (200 Gbps).

- ### CHARACTERISTICS OF TRANSCEIVERS

  - *Bidirectional* transceivers combine and separate data sent over a single fiber. This allows you to send and receive data using a single cable.

  - *Duplex* fiber-optic cable contains two strands of fiber for transmitting and receiving.

TERMINATION POINTS

A termination point is a point where the upstream service enters the building and is distributed throughout the network. These components help keep the central point of the network organized.

- **25 PAIR:** Consists of 25 individual pairs of wires all inside one common insulating jacket. It's often used for telephone cabling and is sometimes called feeder cable because it supplies signal to many connected pairs.

- **66 BLOCK:** This is really only used for old analog telephone connections. It is a standard termination block containing 50 rows.

- **110 BLOCK:** Has largely replaced 66 Block. It's used for RJ-11 as well as RJ-45 connections.

- **PATCH PANEL:** Devices containing a number of connectors, usually of similar type. They are often used in large networks or studios.

- **FIBER DISTRIBUTION PANEL:** These are similar to patch panels, except that they are used for fiber-optic connections.

COPPER CABLE STANDARDS (MOST COMMON TYPES)

CAT3: This cable contains four twisted pair and support up to 15 MHz. It was popular in the mid-1980s but is now obsolete.

CAT5: Also contains four twisted pairs, but is rated for 100 MHz.

CAT5E: This is an enhanced version of Cat 5, it is able to handle disturbance on each pair caused by transmitting over all four at the same time. This is the most popular type used to date.

CAT6: Four twisted wire pairs, rated for 250 MHz, it is often used to connect floors together.

CAT6A: An augmented version of Cat 6. It is rated for 500 MHz and has improved crosstalk characteristics.

CAT7: Four twisted pair rated up to 600 MHz. It has further improved crosstalk characteristics.

RG-6: This is a common coaxial cable type with a 75 ohm impedance.

RG-59: This type is often used for low power video, and has the same resistance as RG-6.

COPPER TERMINATION STANDARDS

TIA/EIA 568A AND 568B: There are two common ways to wire the pins inside a network cable. 568a uses the green pair for pins 1 and 2, but the orange pair is split to pins 3 and 6, separated by the blue pair. In 568b orange is used for 1 and 2, green is used for 3 and 6, separated by blue.

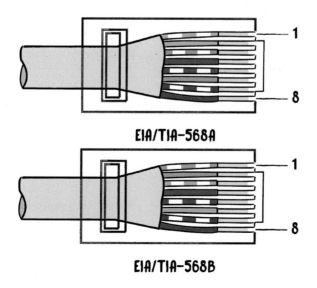

EIA/TIA-568A

EIA/TIA-568B

STRAIGHT-THROUGH & CROSSOVER CABLE: Straight through is a simple connection type where each pin maps to the same pin of the other connector (left image). Crossover cables have pins that "crossover" to other pins of the other connector (right image). Crossover cables are required when connecting like devices (i.e. computer to computer), and straight through cables are used when connecting different types of devices (i.e. a computer to a switch). It is always best to validate the type of cable that is needed to make a connection. Also note that some newer networking devices have the ability to detect the type of required connection and make the change automatically within the device.

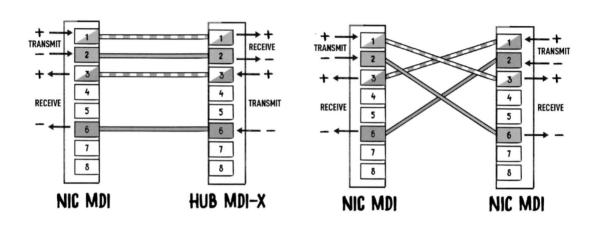

ETHERNET DEPLOYMENT STANDARDS

100BASET: Known as Fast Ethernet uses Cat 5, 5e, or 6 and UTP two-pair wiring. It allows for one user per segment up to 100 meters long, using RJ-45 connectors.

1000BASET: Cat 5, four-pair UTP wiring, up to 100 meters long.

1000BASELX: Single-mode fiber that uses a 9-micron core, 1300 nm laser and can go from 3 km to 10 km.

1000BASESX: Multimode fiber-optic cable, uses 62.6- and 50-micron core, 850 nm laser and goes up to 220 meters 62.6-micron; 550 meters with 50-micron.

10GBASET: A standard created to provide 10 Gbps connections over conventional UTP cables (Cat 5e, 6, and 7). This is the most economical way to implement 10 Gbps links up to 100-meters.

NETWORK DEVICE PLACEMENT

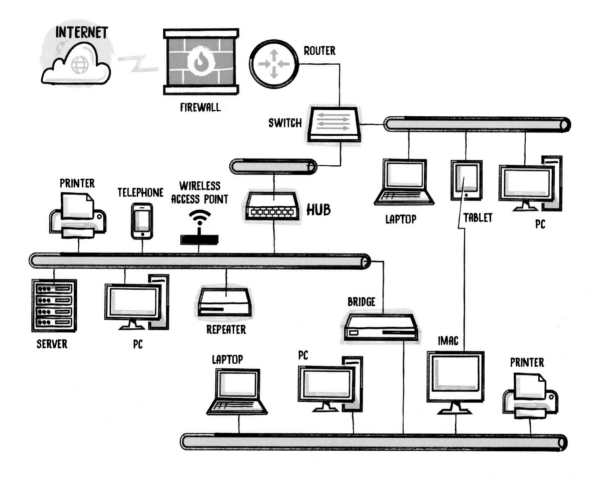

It will be important to be able to determine the correct function and placement of the following network devices as well as how to properly install them in a network.

FIREWALL

Firewalls are imperative to a modern network for protecting its local resources. A firewall can either be a stand-alone device or a software implementation on a server. Whichever you choose, there will be a minimum of two sides to your firewall: a public side that interfaces with the Internet and a private side that interfaces with the network.

It's important to set this up in such a way that all connections between your network and the Internet pass through this firewall. In some cases, you may even want your firewall to filter connections inside your network. Firewalls operate on OSI layer 4 at minimum, but some modern firewalls can operate on OSI layer 7. Firewalls can provide routing functions for a network.

ROUTER

Routers are devices that create the connection between two networks or a network and the Internet. For wireless routers, it's important to place them in an area where their signal will not be easily obstructed. Routers are OSI layer 3 devices.

SWITCH

A switch connects multiple segments of a network together forwarding traffic to the appropriate port. Switches will often be placed somewhere central to the network devices connected to it. The forwarding decisions are the same as on bridges, operating on OSI layer 2, but *multilayer switches* operate on layer 3 and can provide routing functionality.

HUB

Hubs are similar to switches, but less advanced as they forward all traffic out all ports thus having a greater chance for data collisions. They ultimately perform the same function (forwarding data to hosts on the same network) and connect network hosts together in a star topology. A hub will be placed similarly to a switch and operates at OSI layer 1.

BRIDGE

A bridge is a device that connects two similar networks, again much like a switch. It's purpose is to separate collision domains, only allowing data to be sent over if the receiving device is on the other side. You will want to place bridges between the two related networks. Bridges operate on OSI layer 2.

MODEMS

A modem converts analog signal to digital signal. These are commonly used for telephone networks. You might place these in two locations that need to be able to communicate in the event the primary network method goes down as a backup. Modems use OSI layer 2.

WIRELESS ACCESS POINT

This is different from a wireless router in that it makes no routing decisions, it simply allows wireless connections. A WAP is basically a bridge between a wireless network and ethernet network. It's common for these to be placed on each floor of a building to allow connection to the network throughout the building. WAPs, like bridges, are OSI layer 2 devices.

MEDIA CONVERTER

This simply converts one media type to another, i.e. ethernet to fiber-optic. You would place this in any connection that needs to be converted from one type of media to another. Media converters operate at OSI layer 1.

WIRELESS RANGE EXTENDER

This increases the range of the wireless signal and works like a wireless repeater. It's best to place this near the edge of where your wireless signal extends to get the maximum extension. Because a wireless range extender simply repeats a signal, it operates at OSI layer 1.

VOIP ENDPOINT

Voice over IP is a technology that allows phones to be used with software based technology. You would connect this to the network like any other node. VoIP communicates using TCP/UDP/RTP and therefore operates at OSI layer 4.

NETWORK DEVICE INSTALLATION & CONFIGURATION

Now that you know some common network devices and their place in a network, it's good to know how to install and configure these devices.

FIREWALL

How to install a firewall depends on what kind of firewall setup you intend to use, of which there are a few options: A dedicated stand-alone firewall device or a software based firewall running on a server.

A stand-alone firewall will have to be physically setup between your network devices and the Internet just before an outside router, while a software based firewall will commonly be setup with the router. As for configuration, most firewalls default to denying all connections, and it's the job of a network administrator to allow the necessary connections. *Iptables* is a common program used to configure firewall rules on a non-network device (such as a server).

ROUTER

A router should be hooked up to connect multiple networks. It's the responsibility of the router to keep track of the IP addresses and MAC addresses of the devices on its network in a routing table. Common tools for configuring routes are *ip, ifconfig* (deprecated but still in use) and *route*.

MODEMS

To install a modem, you must connect it both to the wall jack (through RJ-11 or coaxial port) and the end device (usually a computer). Modems are not very common today, so chances are if you use one it will be in conjunction with a router. In this case you must also connect the modem to the router. You can often configure a modem by typing in the IP address of the device into your browser to bring up the settings.

VOIP ENDPOINT

The installation and configuration of a VoIP device will depend on the device. Generally you will need to set this up in the same way you configure other network devices, by connecting it to your network via ethernet.

ADVANCED NETWORKING DEVICES

In addition to the devices discussed in the previous two lessons, there are a number of other important devices that are also important.

MULTILAYER SWITCH

A multilayer switch can perform all of the same functions as a regular switch as well as the functions of a router, and at higher speeds. This includes routing between VLANs configured for the switch.

WIRELESS CONTROLLER

A wireless controller, or wireless LAN controller, is a device that manages wireless APs on a network. It automatically configures the settings of Access Points connected to it, including bandwidth and channels.

LOAD BALANCER

A load balancer is a device that distributes traffic load to multiple servers. This is useful if you have a lot of network traffic to access a single resource. You would be able to set up multiple servers with access to that resource and use a load balancer to distribute that traffic.

INTRUSION DETECTION SYSTEM / INTRUSION PREVENTION SYSTEM

An IDS / IPS is a device that scans all of the traffic and devices on a network to detect anomalies and increase the security of your network. An IDS is used to only identify and alert; while an IPS has the same function but with the ability to block the malicious traffic.

PROXY SERVER

A proxy server is a server that makes requests on behalf of a client. These are often used to protect the location of the requesting host from the requested host. These can also be useful for making a request appear like it's coming from another location. A proxy server inside your network for example might allow users to log in and make requests as if they were on the network.

VPN CONCENTRATOR

A Virtual Private Network Concentrator allows VPN tunnels to be created. This is similar to a proxy with the added benefit of encryption. This is more useful for sensitive data.

AAA / RADIUS SERVER

A Remote Authentication Dial-In User Service (RADIUS) is a networking protocol that provides centralized Authentication, Authorization, and Accounting (AAA) services. This is useful for controlling what users have access to your network and who is authorized to use certain features. While AAA/Radius can be used for remote user connections, it is also frequently used in conjunction with managing administrator access to network devices.

UTM APPLIANCE

A Unified Threat Management device is one that combines multiple security features into one device. This might include a firewall, IDS / IPS, gateway, and more. The benefit of this is having your network security more manageable.

NGFW / LAYER 7 FIREWALL

A Next Generation Firewall is a firewall that can operate at Layer 7 of the OSI model. This means a firewall that is able to allow/deny certain applications from communicating as well as only allowing SSL/TLS connections on the browser.

VOIP PBX

A VoIP Private Branch Exchange is a device that manages the connections of VoIP devices, such as phones. This is useful for example in an office where every employee has a VoIP phone and can be reached by an extension.

VOIP GATEWAY

A VoIP Gateway is a device that converts telephony traffic into IP data that can be sent over a network. This is commonly used for a fax machine that requires fax information to be sent over the network.

CONTENT FILTER

A content filter restricts the content that can be accessed via your network. The most common use of this is to prevent employees of a business or students in a school, or even children in a home from accessing potentially explicit or distracting content.

VIRTUALIZATION

Virtualization can be a very helpful part of creating networks. It allows you to overcome some physical limitations such as where devices are placed by providing a logical based network configuration in the form of *virtual machines*.

In a virtual network, each node of the network is represented by a virtual machine. These virtual machines can all be run by one or a few physical devices, allowing an entire network to be set up in one location. This is accomplished by special virtualization software that allows the physical device to share/pool its' resources amongst many virtual servers hosted on it. This is useful for a network that does not need workstations, such as a network of services. For example, a network of web servers may be set up with a virtual machine for each website and a virtual machine for a DNS server and other services. The entire network can then be hosted on a single physical server.

VIRTUAL NETWORKING COMPONENTS

Below are the foundational components to implementing virtualization in your network.

VIRTUAL SWITCH: Forwards packets to the appropriate location like a normal switch, but in the context of a virtual environment. It is a program that switches packets between virtual hosts.

VIRTUAL FIREWALL: VF is a firewall that runs entirely within a virtualized environment and provides the usual firewall functionality in that context.

VIRTUAL NIC: This is a program that allows a computer to connect to a network, rather than just using the physical NIC alone.

VIRTUAL ROUTER: A program that emulates the functionality of a physical router, which is to route and forward packets.

HYPERVISOR: A hypervisor, also known as a Virtual Machine Monitor (VMM), is a software, firmware, or hardware that creates and runs virtual machines. It manages the resources of the virtual machine platforms.

NETWORK STORAGE

STORAGE TYPES

NETWORK ATTACHED STORAGE: NAS is a file-level server connected to a network and is designed for serving files either by its hardware, software, or configuration. It is often built as an appliance or specialized computer.

STORAGE AREA NETWORK: SAN is a network that provides access to consolidated storage. They are normally used to enhance storage devices so that devices appear to the operating system as locally attached devices.

CONNECTION TYPES

FIBRE CHANNEL: A high-speed network technology that provides in-order lossless delivery of data. It's primarily used to connect storage devices in a network.

FIBRE CHANNEL OVER ETHERNET: FCOE is a technology that encapsulates Fibre Channel frames over ethernet networks. It allows the use of high speed ethernet while preserving the Fibre Channel protocol.

INTERNET SMALL COMPUTER SYSTEMS INTERFACE: ISCSI is an internet protocol based storage networking standard for linking together storage facilities. It provides block-level access to devices by carrying SCSI commands over a network.

INFINIBAND: IB is a communications standard for high performance computing that has very high throughput with low latency.

JUMBO FRAME

A jumbo frame is an ethernet frame with more than 1500 bytes of payload (the IEEE 802.3 limit). Jumbos can typically carry up to 9000 bytes of payload. Many private commercial networks can support jumbo frames while most ISPs do not.

WAN TECHNOLOGIES:
SERVICE TYPES & TRANSMISSION MEDIUMS

SERVICE TYPES

INTEGRATED SERVICES DIGITAL NETWORK: ISDN is a circuit-switched telephone network system which provides a set of communication standards for transmitting video, voice, data and other services simultaneously.

T1 / T3: T1 and T3 are versions of a telephone transmission system (T-carrier) created by Bell Laboratories. T1 carries up to 24 calls simultaneously over a single transmission line of copper wire. T3 increases the data rate from 1.544 Mbit/s to 44.736 Mbit/s with 672 channels.

E1 / E3: The E-carrier is a carrier system developed for digital transmission of many simultaneous calls using time-division multiplexing. The E1 specification had a data rate of 2.048 Mbit/s while E3 has a 34.368 Mbit/s data rate.

OC-3 - OC-192: Optical Carrier is a standard for transmitting bandwidth for digital signals over fiber optic networks. Below is a list of the different standards along with their data rates.

NAME	DATA RATE	NOTES
OC-3	155.52 Mbit/s	Also known as STS-3 or STM-1
OC-3c	139.264 Mbit/s	Concatenates 3 OC-1 frames into a single OC-3 alike stream.
OC-12	622.08 Mbit/s	Used by ISPs for WAN connections in an area.
OC-24	1244.16 Mbit/s	Rarely used in commercial deployments
OC-48	2488.32 Mbit/s	This is used as the backbone for many ISPs.
OC-192	9953.28 Mbit/s	A variant of 10 Gigabit Ethernet called WAN PHY is designed to interoperate with this.

DIGITAL SUBSCRIBER LINE: DSL is a high-speed Internet service made for homes and businesses and to compete with cable and other forms of broadband internet. It uses broadband modem technology to allow users to use Internet and phone services over a single line.

METROPOLITAN ETHERNET: Metro ethernet is a MAN based on Ethernet standards. It is used to connect users in a larger service network or the Internet.

CABLE BROADBAND: This is a service that provides Internet using the same infrastructure as cable television. This has been one of the leading forms of residential Internet access but is being caught up to by fiber, wireless, and mobile networks.

DIAL-UP: A form of Internet access that uses facilities of the public switched telephone network (PSTN) to create a connection to ISPs by dialing a telephone number on a conventional telephone line. A modem is used to encode and decode the information.

PRIMARY RATE INTERFACE: PRI is an interface standard used on an ISDN for carrying multiple voice and data transmissions between the network and user. It is a standard for carrying services to enterprises and offices, based on the T1 and E1 standards.

TRANSMISSION MEDIUMS

SATELLITE: Communicates data to a satellite in space and back down to its destination. It is more expensive than other options but supports 1000 Gbit/s download speed and 1000 Mbit/s upload. Satellite can be helpful when other connections by other methods are too difficult.

COPPER: Easy to maintain and inexpensive. It is one of the most popular mediums, but it does have a bandwidth limitation.

FIBER: Has a very high speed and communicates at long distances, but it is more expensive than copper and more difficult to maintain.

WIRELESS: Wireless WANs use the cellular network to provide an Internet connection. This is limited to the coverage of the network.

WAN TECHNOLOGIES:
SERVICE CHARACTERISTICS & TERMINATION

CHARACTERISTICS OF SERVICE

MULTIPROTOCOL LABEL SWITCHING: MPLS is a data-carrying technique for high performance networks. It directs data from one network node to another based on short path labels rather than long network addresses, avoiding routing tables. Labels identify paths between nodes rather than endpoints.

ASYNCHRONOUS TRANSFER MODE: ATM is a communications standard for carrying a range of user traffic such as voice, data, and video. It was also designed for networks that must handle both traditional high-throughput data traffic and real-time low-latency content. ATM is used by PSTN and ISDN.

FRAME RELAY: WAN technology that specifies the physical and data-link layers of channels using a packet switching methodology. It was originally designed for ISDN infrastructure, but is used today in the context of other network interfaces.

POINT-TO-POINT PROTOCOL: PPP is a layer 2 protocol used to establish direct connection between nodes. It connects two routers directly without any middle device. It can provide authentication, encryption, and compression for the connection as well.

POINT-TO-POINT PROTOCOL OVER ETHERNET: PPPOE is a protocol for encapsulating PPP frames inside Ethernet frames. It was originally designed for tunneling packets over the DSL connection to ISP's IP networks.

DYNAMIC MULTIPOINT VIRTUAL PRIVATE NETWORK: DMVPN is a tunneling form of VPN supported by certain routers and Unix-like operating systems. It creates a dynamic-mesh VPN network without having to pre-configure all possible endpoints by statically configuring devices as hubs and the connections between them as spokes. No new configuration is needed to add new spokes and a tunnel can be created on-demand without any configuration.

SIP TRUNKING: VoIP technology based on Session Initiation Protocol (SIP). It allows Internet Telephony Service Providers (ITSPs) to deliver services like telephone and unified communications to customers. The applications include voice, video, desktop sharing, web conferencing, and more.

TERMINATION

DEMARCATION POINT: The demarcation point, sometimes called demarc or DMARC, is the point where the service provider's network ends and connects with the customer's on-premises wiring. It decides who is responsible for wiring at a given point: the provider or the customer.

CHANNEL SERVICE UNIT / DATA SERVICE UNIT (CSU/DSU): CSU / DSU is a device used to connect equipment, such as a router, to a digital circuit, such as a T1 line. The CSU part is in charge of the connection to the network while the DSU is responsible for interfacing with the device (i.e., router).

SMART JACK: A smart jack is a type of Network Interface Device that is able to provide more complicated types of telecommunication services such as signal conversion, converting codes and protocols, buffer/regenerate signals, and more.

NETWORK OPERATIONS

NETWORK OPERATIONS

Operating a network requires a diverse and ever-growing set of skills. Communicating how the network is set up, planning for disasters, baselining the network, and responding to incidents are all routine parts of a network administrator's responsibilities. This section will equip you with a basic understanding of each of those responsibilities, so that you can grow your skillset as a network administrator.

The first part of this section goes over network diagrams: the basic symbols that are used, the difference between logical and physical diagrams, and accompanying documentation.

Next we will cover business continuity *aka* how to keep the network running and customers happy. Availability and disaster recovery are the two primary concepts covered.

The last half of this section will be devoted to processes, policies, and best practices. Monitoring the network, understanding the rules around what users and organizations are able to do, and our primary focus will be best practices for operating and securing the network.

DIAGRAMS

Diagrams are an important part of networking for documentation purposes and clarity. Below are some of the most common diagram devices used.

DIAGRAM SYMBOLS

A common diagram used in networking is called a *network diagram*. This is a diagram that shows each device on a network as well as how it is connected with the other devices. To represent the devices you will use these symbols:

 HUB: Represented by a box with an arrow on top that spans the whole length.

 ROUTER: Represented with a cylinder with four arrows on top. Two point inward at each other, and the other two, which are perpendicular to the first, point outward away from each other.

 WORKGROUP SWITCH: Represented by a box with four arrows on top. The arrows start in the middle of the box and alternate directions, left and right.

  FIREWALL: A firewall is depicted as a brick wall.

 IP PHONE: An IP phone is represented by a phone icon with the letters "IP" on it.

LAYER 3 SWITCH: This is shown as a box with a circle in the center of the face, and arrows pointing originating at the circle and spanning to the edges.

 ACCESS POINT: Depicted as a box with waves on the front face.

 ATM SWITCH: An ATM Switch is represented by a box with two double sided arrows that span the length of the box, crossing over each other to form an X.

LOGICAL VS PHYSICAL DIAGRAMS

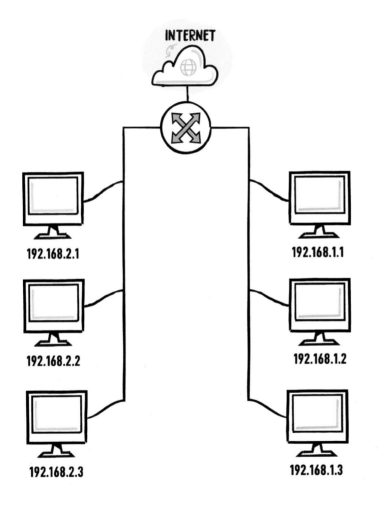

INTERNET

192.168.2.1

192.168.2.2

192.168.2.3

192.168.1.1

192.168.1.2

192.168.1.3

Logical diagrams are a type of network diagram that shows the relationship between components of a network. This might not include how one device is physically connected to another, but if data is shared between two devices then a link is likely to be shown. This type of diagram is used to give people who are unfamiliar with your network an idea of how it is configured.

Logical Diagram

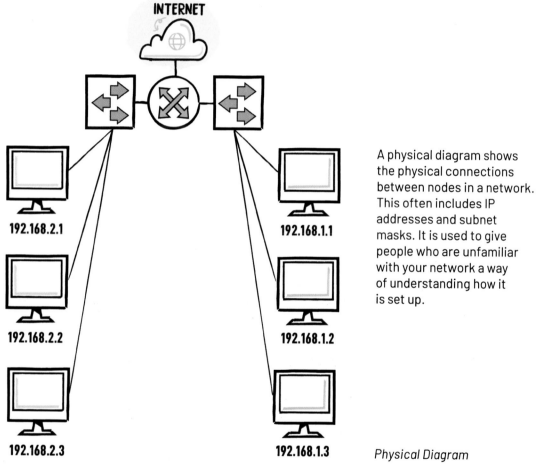

INTERNET

192.168.2.1

192.168.2.2

192.168.2.3

192.168.1.1

192.168.1.2

192.168.1.3

A physical diagram shows the physical connections between nodes in a network. This often includes IP addresses and subnet masks. It is used to give people who are unfamiliar with your network a way of understanding how it is set up.

Physical Diagram

Notice that the physical diagram displays the switch that each group is connected to. However, in a logical diagram this is not necessary because the switch does not affect how the network operates with the router.

RACK DIAGRAM

A Rack Diagram shows the physical layout of equipment within a rack. It's a way of showing a third party exactly which component of the rack you are referencing, and also allows for the proper planning of space and power needed for equipment within a datacenter.

OTHER DOCUMENTATION

Companies with networks as a part of their infrastructure will often have (or need) operating procedures and instructions. It is important to have procedures for the following things.

CHANGE MANAGEMENT: Changes to the network can introduce risks by accidentally disabling or breaking another part of the network. It is important that you have a procedure for how changes, such as upgrades and configurations, should be implemented to avoid mistakes. Have a fallback plan for mistakes.

CABLE MANAGEMENT: ANSI / TIA / EIA 606. This is the standard for how to document your network; mapping it out, identifying cables used to connect the network, color coding, etc. You should document and label all cables and ports in your network.

SYSTEM LABELING: Always label all servers and workstations using a clearly visible UID system.

CIRCUIT LABELING: You should label all components of the WAN. This includes the Demarc interface, CSU/DSU and the router connected to the CSU/DSU. The label information should include the WAN provider circuit ID, phone number, and an internal reference name.

PATCH PANEL LABELING: There is not a lot of space for documentation on a patch panel, but it is important to know which port on the panel maps to which port on the floor.

BASELINE: Keep track of the performance of your network over time to have data which you can make decisions with.

INVENTORY MANAGEMENT: Keep a record of every asset you have. This is helpful to keep track of all of the devices at your disposal as well as accurate financial records.

BUSINESS CONTINUITY: AVAILABILITY & DISASTER RECOVERY

Business continuity involves consistently maintaining operations throughout the business' lifetime. Generally, this is understood to mean maximizing uptime (availability), and minimizing downtime (disaster recovery). Business continuity processes can bear significant costs for a business, especially those centered around fault tolerance and high availability. Any business looking to implement the concepts below should weigh the risk of downtime against the cost of maintaining this infrastructure.

AVAILABILITY CONCEPTS

FAULT TOLERANCE: The ability of a system to maintain uptime despite the failure of one or more pieces of hardware in that system. Fault tolerant systems strive for *zero* downtime by detecting issues and switching to backup systems should the need arise.

HIGH AVAILABILITY: Similar to *Fault Tolerance*, but a little more forgiving. High availability systems are focused on recovering from failures very quickly, rather than silently switching over to backup systems. Typically, high availability can refer to hardware- and software-based systems, while fault tolerance refers almost exclusively to hardware systems. In addition, high availability systems take geographic location into account; local events (e.g. weather) can take one site offline while a site in a different geographic location can maintain operations.

LOAD BALANCING: Configuring multiple devices (servers, NICs, etc.) to share traffic between each other. Many high availability web applications will load balance requests across several servers to minimize the chance the application becomes overloaded and downtime occurs.

CLUSTERING: Clustering involves combining two or more physical devices into one logical device. Clustering is an essential component of business continuity as it tightly couples primary and backup devices and can be used to enable fault tolerance, high availability, and load balancing.

NIC TEAMING: Assigning multiple physical NICs to a single virtual network adapter. Network access will not be disrupted if a physical NIC fails, because the virtual adapter will silently load balance between the other working NICs.

PORT AGGREGATION: Combining multiple switch ports into one logical port. This technique offers redundancy, in case of port failure, and increased bandwidth through load balancing of network traffic. You may also see this referred to as *Link Aggregation*.

POWER MANAGEMENT: Power management involves maintaining and recovering power in the event of an outage.

- **BATTERY BACKUPS / UPS:** Battery backups and UPSes (Uninterruptible Power Supply) are systems that, like the name says, automatically provide power to critical systems *uninterrupted* in the event of a power failure.

- **POWER GENERATORS:** These are self-contained systems that can generate power for short periods of time.

- **DUAL POWER SUPPLIES:** Offer a failover option if one supply experiences downtime.

- **REDUNDANT CIRCUITS:** Like dual power supplies, redundant circuits offer a failover option if one network circuit experiences downtime.

RECOVERY CONCEPTS

BACKUPS: Data backups are an important concept in disaster recovery, as you'll see below. There are a few different implementations:

- **FULL:** A full backup copies every piece of data available in a system. It is the simplest idea, but requires the most storage space and time to backup.

- **DIFFERENTIAL:** Differential backups only copy the data that has been changed since the last full backup. Taken together, full and differential backups will accumulate to reconstruct the current state of your system.

- **INCREMENTAL:** Incremental backups only copy the data that has been changed since the last incremental backup. Just like differential backups, incremental backups can reconstruct the current state of your system.

BACKUP SITES: If a disaster happens, backup sites offer a way for a business to continue working while the normal site is recovering. There are three different types of backup sites corresponding to the amount of effort it would take to get the site operational.

- **COLD SITES:** A bare-minimum backup site; generally just a building and limited equipment. Cold sites require significant setup time, but are the cheapest to maintain.

- **WARM SITES:** A semi-ready backup site. Warm sites generally have some hardware already set up, but they require additional configuration and setup before they are ready.

- **HOT SITES:** Hot sites are the most expensive backup sites to maintain. These sites require minimal setup before a business can start using them, because they have been pre-configured with the same setup as the normal business environment. They may only require the very latest data to get back online.

SLA, MTTR, & MTBF

SLA REQUIREMENTS: SLA stands for "Service-Level Agreement". An SLA is a contract between an entity and service provider, detailing which services will be provided, under what conditions those services will be provided, and additional steps should either party violate the contract. For example, many businesses define SLA's with their vendors, such as Internet providers. Examples of an SLA with an ISP would include the expected latency and bandwidth of the internet circuits provided, as well as the amount of allowable downtime and expected resolution times. The more stringent the SLA, the higher the cost of service.

MTBF: Shorthand for "Mean Time Between Failures". This measurement represents the average time between failures that put a device out of service. MTBF can be calculated with the following:
(total device uptime) / (total number of device failures)

MTTR: Shorthand for "Mean Time to Repair". This measurement represents the average time it takes to repair a device which has failed. MTTR can be calculated with the following:
(total repair time) / (total number of times repaired)

SCANNING & MONITORING PROCESSES

MONITORING PROCESSES

LOG REVIEWING: During operation, processes on a system will log their activity. It's important to keep enough storage space to store all of these logs. To simplify your logs, it's a good idea to keep your logs "rolled up" in samples of certain time intervals. From this log data you can create graphs to better interpret the data.

PORT SCANNING: One way to monitor your network is to monitor the connections on each port. Nmap is a common tool for this. Nmap can query a device and tell you which ports are open or closed, analyze its operating system, see services running on it, and run custom scripts.

VULNERABILITY SCANNING: A vulnerability scanner can show you the potential vulnerabilities on a system. They can find unknown devices on a network, and should be run from inside and outside of your network. This utility can also show you what security controls/patches are missing, or where misconfigurations exist.

PATCH MANAGEMENT: If vulnerability is found on your network, it is often necessary to apply a software *patch* to the vulnerable system. Patches provide stability and security to your network. It's a good idea to apply patches as soon as they are released and before you find vulnerability.

- **ROLLBACK:** If a patch breaks something in your system or network, you may want to unpatch, or *rollback*, to the older version of your software.

REVIEWING BASELINES: After collecting monitoring information, you can form a baseline. A baseline shows you what "normal" operating of your network looks like, and any variation from that could be ground for investigating your network.

PACKET/TRAFFIC ANALYSIS: Using a protocol analyzer, you can collect packets on your network and identify unknown traffic, or anything that is out of place.

EVENT MANAGEMENT

It's important to know whether your interfaces are up or down on a device. This can be determined by simply pinging the interface (or using SNMP to gather more in depth information) and is usually done automatically. When an interface or service goes down, it is important to notify the correct people either by creating a ticket, email or SMS. You also want to create reports showing the uptime of services over time.

A Security Information and Event Management (SIEM) platform allows you to collect information from security events and send out alerts in real-time. A SIEM platform will usually offer short and long term reports and allow you to create custom reports.

SNMP MONITORS

A Simple Network Management Protocol (SNMP) queries devices and returns details about how a device is performing. This data is stored in a Management Information Base (MIB). In version 3 of SNMP, you can collect bulk data from the MIB in a secure fashion.

METRICS

Metrics can help you locate problems in devices on your network. MIB-II is a standard that allows you to monitor the metrics of a device at any time. It can tell you if an interface is up or down, error rates, what error is occurring, traffic or utilization of an interface, packets dropped, and bandwidth details.

PATCHING PROCESSES

Patching systems on your network is the most reliable way of preventing the exploitation of a vulnerability. In general, it's a good idea to apply updates as soon as they are available to your system or application, but this must be weighed against ensuring that you validate and test patches before pushing them out to an entire enterprise. Furthermore, larger environments will implement patch repositories, which have the ability to download patches and push them out to applicable systems on a scheduled basis. Below are instructions on how to perform basic updates on each operating system.

WINDOWS

On Windows, updates can be applied from the system settings. Searching "update" on modern versions of Windows will allow you to find this dialog.

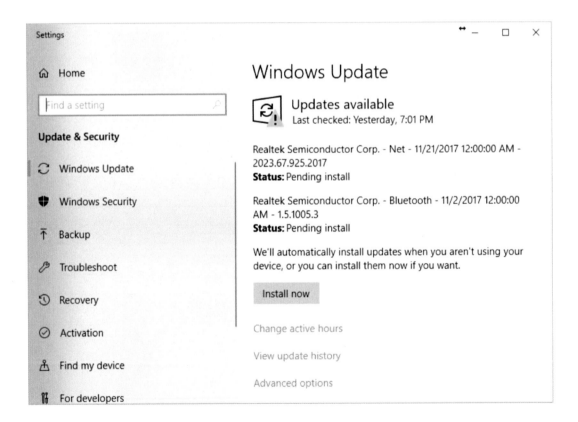

MAC

On Mac, updates are handled from the App Store. This includes app and system updates.

	Software Update	Updates are available for your computer	
	Restart Required ○	Command Line Tools (macOS High Sierra version 10.13) for Xcode 9.3, Command Line Tools (macOS High Sierra version 10.13) for Xcode 9.4, iTunes 12.7.5, macOS 10.13.2 Update Combo 10.13.2 More	UPDATE

UNIX

To apply updates on Unix-like operating systems, you will need to use the system's *package manager*. Below are the update statements for some of the most popular package managers, with *apt* or *apt-get* being the most popular for debian linux.

APT   *$ apt upgrade or apt-get upgrade*

EQUO   *$ equo upgrade --ask*

YARN   *$ yarn upgrade*

YUM   *$ yum update*

        NOTE: The $ denotes a terminal command.

REMOTE ACCESS

Remote access is a key component to most organizations today. As companies look to further enable remote/telework, capabilities must be put in place to allow employees to access corporate resources when not physically sitting in their home office. Remote access is also a key method utilized by IT staff for managing their company's infrastructure while not on site. For instance, a network operations center (NOC) that is centralized might utilize various remote access technologies to administer and manage equipment at their remote offices. Below are some of the methods and tools that may be utilized by remote users and/or IT administrators.

VPN

VPN provides a secure way of accessing resources by routing requests through another device and encrypting the connection.

INTERNET PROTOCOL SECURITY: IPSEC is a protocol that encrypts and signs each packet sent.

SSL / TLS: Common encryption protocols used to send secure data over a VPN connection.

SITE-TO-SITE: In this method, a VPN appliance is set up on any two networks that want to communicate, which encrypts the data before sending it over the Internet to the other VPN appliance. The appliance then decrypts it and sends it to the destination.

CLIENT-TO-SITE: Software is installed on a client machine which allows a connection to a VPN Concentrator on the network being connected to.

REMOTE DESKTOP PROTOCOL

RDP is a form of remote access allows you to interact with a Windows server or PC as if you were sitting at it. RDP clients exist for many operating systems. TeamViewer is a popular RDP program that is free to use.

VIRTUAL NETWORK COMPUTING

VNC is remote desktop software that uses Remote Frame Buffer (RFB) protocol, and is open source. A popular open source VNC program is TigerVNC.

SSH

Secure Shell is used to connect to another machine securely and access a terminal. It operates much like Telnet with added security. SSH can be installed using a package manager on Unix operating systems or via the web on Windows. A popular Windows SSH client is called Putty.

WEB-BASED MANAGEMENT CONSOLE

This provides an easy to use interface for device management. In this case you simply log in to a management webpage to perform operations. This may not provide a comprehensive selection of operations to perform however.

REMOTE FILE ACCESS

FTP: File Transfer Protocol allows you to perform many file operations and provides authentication. A popular FTP client is called FileZilla.

FTPS: A secure version of FTP that uses SSL to secure the connection.

SFTP: Also a secure version of FTP, it performs the same functions with added SSH security.

TFTP: A simple version of FTP that's easier to use but is less capable. Solarwinds is a popular TFTP program.

OUT-OF-BAND MANAGEMENT

Remote access when the network is unavailable.

USB: As long as you are inside the network, a USB connection can be used in place of the network connection.

MODEM: A modem connection can be used when the network is down as a backup means of connecting to the network.

CONSOLE ROUTER: In the event of a network outage, you may have some key components connected to a console router or comm server. This allows you to connect remotely to the comm server and from there choose where to connect.

POLICIES - USERS

PRIVILEGED USER AGREEMENT

A Privileged User Agreement specifies what a user does and does not have access to in a network. This holds users responsible for accessing data that they should not access and protects users when accessing data they do have access to.

Network administrators will have nearly complete access and are expected to use the lowest-privilege possible for accomplishing a task. They are also expected to have high ethical standards. Signing a Privileged User Agreement means that you will hold the highest level of professionalism and confidentiality toward the company.

ACCEPTABLE USE POLICIES

The AUP details how an employee can interact with the devices on the network. It should have details on every device on the network and cover many topics such as Internet use, phone use, local storage use and more. An AUP will limit the legal liability of a company in the event something goes wrong because of a misused device.

NON-DISCLOSURE AGREEMENT POLICIES

An NDA is an agreement between two parties that ensures one party does not disclose information to another party that is not authorized to have access. An NDA can be created internally between a company and an employee, or externally between a company and a third party company / contractor, or between two independent parties that are sharing proprietary information related to an idea, system, process, or methodology that they believe to be unique or not publicly available.

POLICIES: ORGANIZATIONAL

LICENSING RESTRICTIONS

There is almost always a license associated with a piece of hardware, an application, or an operating system. It's important to have all licenses up to date to avoid having devices become unavailable. Be sure to document and keep track of licenses.

BRING YOUR OWN DEVICE POLICIES

Bring Your Own Device (BYOD) policies are important because they detail how an employee should handle their personal devices when they are also used for business. When company and personal information is stored on the same device, it is important to keep company data safe while not violating the privacy of the employee.

SYSTEM LIFE CYCLE

The system life cycle is the overall process a company uses to identify, build, integrate, optimize and remove technologies within their environment. Each company may have a different overall process, but most life cycles have similar key points:

- Identifying business/operational needs that would require IT technologies
- Analyzing current IT environment and tools to see if something available can meet the requirement
- Designing/developing the technical solution
- Testing the solution
- Installing and integrating the solution
- Operations and maintenance
- Solution improvement / upgrades
- Solution termination (sunsetting / disposal)

One key area that organizations should definitely be cognizant of from a policy perspective is disposal. When a device is no longer usable by the company, a procedure should be in place for managing that asset or disposing of it. This may include outdated or broken PCs, laptops, tablets and more. When creating these policies, it is important to check with the legal team in the event that there are legal restrictions to how things can be disposed of. For example, certain data may be required to be stored by law and your procedures and policies should align with this.

In addition to legal restrictions, it is not a good practice to allow critical information to be thrown away. If important company data is in the trash it can be picked up by a stranger creating a potential security issue.. The best way to dispose of data is to physically destroy the media.

BEST PRACTICES: OPERATIONS

ON-BOARDING / OFF-BOARDING PROCEDURES

It is important when a new user is being added to the network that they understand the policies and procedures regarding network use. This might include reading the employee handbook or a separate AUP. Users will also need accounts created for them and proper privileges assigned to them. Along with accounts and access, they will also need the proper hardware assigned. Procedures are also required for off-boarding, or when somebody moves to a different department. This process should be pre-planned so that you are prepared. This process will include restoring any hardware given to the user, removing their user account and/or changing its privileges, and saving any data that the user may have that is important to the company. All of these processes should be well documented.

DATA LOSS PREVENTION

It is extremely vital that you know where the data in your network is being stored, especially for sensitive data such as Social Security numbers, credit card numbers, or medical records. Detailed policies and procedures should be in place outlining how sensitive data is transferred and encrypted. You should be aware of unique protocols, compliance requirements, and specific standards that your organization may follow.

DLP technologies can be deployed on a network to validate that data is being transferred and stored in a way that aligns with company policies. If there is a violation, an alert can be sent to an administrator or other person in charge.

INTERNATIONAL EXPORT CONTROLS

If any data needs to be sent to a company outside of your country, there are often regulations that control how those transactions can take place. This applies not only to hardware being exported, but also software and data. It is important to have explicit documentation for what hardware, software, and data can and cannot leave the country, and under what circumstances.

Different types of software and hardware may have different export rules. For example, it may be necessary to have a different protocol for software that can be of military use or for hacking. Be sure that your policies comply with local and federal laws as well as the foreign laws of the nation you are exporting to by checking with your legal team.

INCIDENT RESPONSE POLICIES

Although many preventive measures can be taken, it's possible that a security incident may still occur. In this event, it is important that you have a detailed policy on how to react. This could include a user falling victim to a phishing attack, a DDoS attack, or stolen passwords. It is best to be as specific as possible and think of these situations ahead of time.

Your network should have an automated monitoring system that is constantly searching for these issues and reporting them if and when they occur. After identifying an attack, you should categorize the attack so that you can see how to respond. Each category should lead to a procedure, which should have been created ahead of time.

BEST PRACTICES: SECURITY

PASSWORD POLICY

A password policy is a written policy that specifies when passwords should be updated. The higher the level of security, the more frequently users will have to change passwords. Password recovery procedures should not be trivial so as to prevent unauthorized password recoveries.

Most companies will require their employees' passwords to be changed every 60 days, but this can be much more frequent when users have access to more sensitive data.

REMOTE ACCESS POLICIES

A Remote Access Policy will outline how to manage remote access to the network. This applies to employees and third parties who need to access your network from a remote location. The RAP should specify the encryption used and the hardware/software requirements, ensure confidentiality, and detail who is allowed to access the network.

SAFETY PROCEDURES & POLICIES

Safety procedures and policies are another important aspect of working with and around your network. This will ensure employees use the network safely and the company is not liable for actions that violate these policies. These policies might include electrical safety, clothing safety, fire safety, toxic waste safety, and others. A Material Safety Data Sheet (MSDS) outlines all of these policies and should also adhere to local and federal laws.

BEYOND NETWORK+
For more in-depth information on NIST password standards check out **pages.nist.gov/800-63-3/sp800-63b.html#sec5**

NETWORK SECURITY

NETWORK SECURITY

Unfortunately, the expansion of computer networks has also led to an increase in computer crimes and misuses. Every device exposed to the Internet is routinely scanned for open services in the hopes that they can be exploited by cyber criminals. To keep their networks safe, network administrators must be mindful of common network attacks and appropriately apply mitigations and defenses to thwart these attacks. This section will cover such attacks and the strategies for defending against them.

The first part of this section covers physical security, because not all security threats operate entirely on the network. Network authentication, access control, and wireless security are covered next. Then, we will get into common network attacks - what they are and how they work.

Finally, device hardening and mitigation techniques will round out this section. Both network- and policy-based mitigation techniques will be covered, because the best way to mitigate security risk is through a combination of technical and administrative controls.

PHYSICAL SECURITY DEVICES

There are many ways an attacker might try to take advantage of your network, and not all of them include remotely hacking your network. It is equally important to consider physical security when you are attempting to secure your environment. Below are some of the most common physical security measures that you should be familiar with.

DETECTION

When a physical security breach occurs, you should be able to identify that breach with one of the following methods.

MOTION DETECTION: A motion detector can allow you to know if an individual enters a certain area. It will not allow you to see who it is, but it is useful for areas that are off-limit to anybody.

VIDEO SURVEILLANCE: Sometimes called CCTV (closed circuit television), video surveillance can act as many security guards covering multiple angles. It is important to consider the requirements for the camera before installation.

ASSET TRACKING TAGS: This is a physical tag that you put on the components owned by your organization. You can keep a database of your assets associated with these tags.

TAMPER DETECTION: When there are too many items to keep track of, it is beneficial to have assets that can detect tampering such as case sensors, alarms, or foil asset tags.

PREVENTION

Detection is great in order to know when attacks occur, but your first consideration should be prevention. You can often prevent simple breaches with the following measures.

BADGES: All employees can be made to wear an ID badge at all times. This badge will have information such as a picture, name, and other employment details. You can even use certain badges for door access chipped cards. Be sure to train all employees to look for IDs and ask questions if they don't see one.

BIOMETRICS: This is a form of authentication that uses a biological part of you to identify you such as an iris or fingerprint. Biometrics are nearly impossible to change.

SMART CARDS: Can be integrated with devices to allow access to certain users.

KEY FOBS: Generates a pseudo-random authentication code for you to get access to something.

LOCKS: This is one of the most basic types of security. A simple lock with a key required to gain access, or possibly a lock that requires a card or key fob.

AUTHENTICATION

AUTHORIZATION, AUTHENTICATION, & ACCOUNTING

The AAA framework consists of three parts: accounting, authentication, and authorization. The following is a list of technologies for applying AAA to your network.

RADIUS: Remote Authentication Dial-in User Service (RADIUS) is a common AAA protocol that supports a variety of platforms and devices. It provides a centralized authentication system which allows you to use your credentials to log in to many parts of the network such as the router, firewall, or workstation.

TACACS+: Terminal Access Controller Access-Control System (TACACS+) is like RADIUS but it was originally developed for Cisco products and fully encrypts the payload of the packets. It also allows for greater granularity on the TACACs server for authorization of specific commands on the remote devices. Even though it was developed for Cisco, it now has wider vendor support.

RADIUS	TACACS+
UDP 1812, 1645 (Authentication), 1813, 1646 (Accounting	TCP 49
Created by IETF, Open Standard	Created by Cisco, Open Standard
Password Only	Full Packet Encryption
Unidirectional CHAP	Bidirectional CHAP
Low resource dependent	Requires more resources
No command logging	Full logging of commands
Used for network access	Supports administration
Authentication and Authorization is combined. Accounting is separate	Authentication, Authorization and accounting are separate.
Extensive accounting	Limited Accounting
Priviledge mode is supported	15 priviledge modes are supported

KERBEROS: Kerberos is a network authentication protocol that allows you to authenticate once and be trusted throughout the system via the use of tickets. It uses encryption that prevents man-in-the-middle attacks and replay attacks.

SINGLE SIGN-ON: SSO is a feature of an authentication system that allows you to sign in once and be trusted from then on. This isn't supported by every device on a network however so additional authentication may be required.

LOCAL AUTHENTICATION: This is a decentralized authentication method which stores the credentials on the device you are logging in to. Most devices require a local account which the administrator should have access to.

LDAP: Lightweight Directory Access Protocol (LDAP) is a protocol for reading and writing directories on a network. It is used to keep track of objects in a database which can be queried for resources. LDAP forms a hierarchical structure that can be searched for objects.

CERTIFICATES: Using public and private keys, a certificate can be created for an employee or user to allow them to gain access to resources. For example, an ID card, key fob, or a certificate on a personal device.

AUDITING AND LOGGING: All login attempts made on a network should be logged and audits made to see how resources are being used and if your applications are still secure. You can also create time-of-day restrictions that limit when logins can be made to the network.

MULTI-FACTOR AUTHENTICATION

Multi-Factor Authentication requires multiple means of authentication before granting you access to resources. This makes unauthorized access much less common because it is very unlikely that an attacker can have multiple of your authentication methods. Multi-Factor Authentication will always require you to provide at least two of the following:

SOMETHING YOU KNOW: This may be a password, your birthday, a PIN number or anything else that you know in your head.

SOMETHING YOU HAVE: This may be an ID card, a key, a USB drive, or any other personal article used for identification.

SOMETHING YOU ARE: This is something biological about you, including a fingerprint or iris.

SOMEWHERE YOU ARE: This uses your geographical location during authentication. This may use your IPv4 address or GPS.

SOMETHING YOU DO: A unique action that you do, such as a signature, or typing styles. This is similar to biometrics but is external to the person.

ACCESS CONTROL

In a network where users require authentication, it is important to implement a way of keeping users off of the network until the user is authorized to access it. Below are the most common ways of implementing this.

NETWORK ACCESS CONTROL

NAC refers to the implementation of an access control system. A NAC ensures only authorized users are accessing the network.

IEEE 802.1X

Port based access control. This refers to physical interfaces, which enables and disables ports based on authentication (usually authenticated with EAP and RADIUS). For better security, it is good to keep any unused ports disabled and check frequently for duplicate MAC addresses on the network to stop spoofing. 802.1X uses three devices for this process: the *supplicant*, which contacts the *authenticator*, which passes the login to the *authentication server*. If the credentials match what is shown in the authentication server, the supplicant is given access.

PORT SECURITY

This prevents unauthorized devices from connecting, and can alert a user or disable the port when a MAC address doesn't match what is allowed for that port.

MAC FILTERING

The MAC address is a unique hardware address for a device, which can be used to filter which devices can and cannot access the network.

CAPTIVE PORTALS

This is very common on wireless networks. If your device is not recognized on the network, you are provided with a login screen where you can authenticate.

ACCESS CONTROL LISTS

ACLs are used to allow or deny traffic by examining the packets being sent. These are usually applied to routers or switch interfaces. ACLs evaluate on certain criteria, filtering on IP addresses or port numbers.

WIRELESS SECURITY

In modern networks, wireless security is an extremely important part of keeping your network safe. To do this, you should be familiar with the following technologies.

ENCRYPTION METHODS

WPA: Wi-Fi Protected Access, the follow-up to Wired Equivalent Privacy (WEP), uses Temporal Key Integrity Protocol (TKIP) where every packet gets a unique 128-bit encryption key and the Initialization Vector (IV) is larger and an encrypted hash.

TKIP-RC4: TKIP mixed keys plus a sequence counter to prevent replay attacks. It implemented a 64-bit integrity check, but had its own vulnerabilities and was eventually abandoned.

WPA2: Replaced WPA in 2004. It uses CCMP-AES to encrypt data. Additional resources are required to take advantage of WPA2.

CCMP-AES: Advanced Encryption Standard replaces TKIP and uses a 128-bit key and block size.

AUTHENTICATION AND AUTHORIZATION

EAP: Extensible Authentication Protocol is a framework for allowing users to authenticate to a network. WPA and WPA2 both use forms of EAP to provide authentication.

- PEAP: Protective EAP (created by Cisco, Microsoft, RSA) encapsulates EAP within a TLS tunnel.

- EAP-FAST: FAST stands for Flexible Authentication via Secure Tunneling. EAP-FAST is lightweight and secure.

- EAP-TLS: EAP with TLS for encryption which provides strong security. Most of the security industry uses this type.

SHARED OR OPEN: This is when no authentication is required for your network.

PRE-SHARED KEY: A common password for all users who are authenticating. This is very common for home routers using WPA2.

MAC FILTERING: This method authenticates a user based on their MAC address, checking it against a list of authorized users.

GEOFENCING: This uses geographical location to control features of a network. One example is a network in which cameras are disabled when somebody is at work, but this method can also be used to authenticate users by only allowing logins when the device is near a particular area.

COMMON NETWORK ATTACKS

To prepare for potential attacks on your network, you should familiarize yourself with common attack methods.

DOS

An attack in which the attacker makes a service unavailable is called a Denial of Service (DoS). This is often done by taking advantage of a design flaw, vulnerability, or by overloading the traffic to that service.

A DoS can happen unintentionally if you don't have enough bandwidth of system resources to support your traffic, causing a service to become unresponsive. For example, if the power goes out in your building, this would cause a DoS. A Distributed DoS (DDoS) occurs when the requests overload your service from many different sources. This makes detecting the attack much harder.

A reflection attack happens when an attacker spoofs the source address of request packets in order to pretend to be the host that they are attacking. Servers are unable to distinguish legitimate versus spoofed requests, so the service replies directly to the victim. This technique keeps the attacker's real IP address hidden from both the victim and the reflected device.

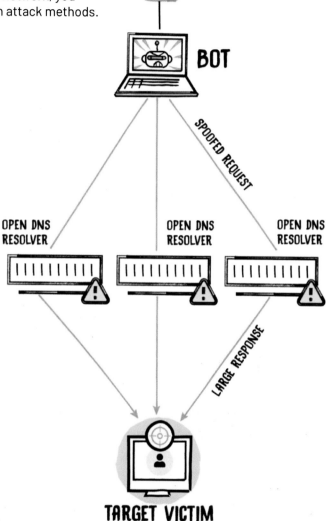

An amplification attack is similar to a reflection attack, but the reply from the service is much bigger than the request. This means that the attacker can overwhelm the victim's machine if using the right service or type of service request. The larger the difference between the size of the request and the response is called the amplification factor.

SOCIAL ENGINEERING

Social Engineering is the art of exploiting human psychology rather than directly exploiting a vulnerability in a piece of technology. Instead, Social Engineering involves an attacker using social interaction to gain access to a system, network, building or data. This may include a phone call where the attacker impersonates an authorized user, or an email asking for your credentials. The attacker will pretend to have authority, or intimidate others, or show consensus that they have permission to the information in question. Social Engineers will try to make you believe that the situation needs to be handled promptly so you provide the information or access without thinking through the policies or procedures that may be in place to prevent such access.).

INSIDER THREAT

With an insider threat, the attacker is given access by the company because they are employed or have been approved by the company to be there (such as a Contractor or Approved Vendor). Someone inside the company already has more information and access than somebody on the outside. To minimize the threat of data loss or attacks from insiders, only grant the minimum permission required for their job, and have strict procedures for sharing information.

Typically employees/contractors/approved vendors are trusted by the company, but sometimes these attacks can occur when they are careless, when they are scammed out of information, when they are blackmailed, or if they become disgruntled.

LOGIC BOMB

A logic bomb is a type of malware that waits for an event to occur to perform its attack. They are often set for a certain time to attack; deleting files or denying service. Logic bombs are almost always unique to the system they are on, so it is important to have formal change control to detect when things change on a system.

ROGUE ACCESS POINT

A rogue access point is a significant potential backdoor. Attackers will plug a WAP into your network and configure it to allow unrestricted connections. To prevent this type of attack, you should schedule periodic surveys where you walk around looking for devices or use other devices such as a Wi-Fi Pineapple.

EVIL TWIN

A Wireless Evil Twin is an AP that is connected and configured exactly the same as your other APs. The evil twin will act as your AP and allow users to connect, at which point they can see the data being sent back and forth.

WAR DRIVING

War driving combines Wi-Fi monitoring and a GPS. This is a method of driving around and gathering Wi-Fi information.

PHISHING

Phishing is a technique used to convince users to give up personal information. It is a mixture of social engineering and spoofing. Examples of this might be fake password recovery emails, fake login pages, fake payment pages, or any other means of tricking you into releasing sensitive information. The best defense against this is training your employees to detect phishing attacks by looking at the URL and other website identifiers.

Spear phishing is when an attacker uses inside information to make their phishing more believable and is usually directed to a small group of people.

RANSOMWARE

Ransomware is a type of malware that takes control of your system and only releases control to you when you pay the attacker a certain amount of money. Certain types of ransomware are fake and don't actually take control of your system, these can be removed by any IT professional. A new generation of ransomware, called crypto-malware, encrypts all of the data on your computer and only applies a decryption key when the payment is made to the attacker. It is important to always have a backup of your data and keep your operating systems up to date.

DNS POISONING

DNS poisoning occurs when the information is modified in a DNS server. If an attacker can modify the DNS records, they can redirect the service's users to different servers. For example, if your network's DNS record for *chase.com* is modified to point to a fake bank website, it can cause users to give their bank information to the attacker.

SPOOFING

Spoofing is the method of one device or person pretending to be another device or person. A popular attack is email address spoofing, where an attacker makes their email appear to come from a trusted source. Caller ID spoofing is another popular method, where the attacker makes a phone call appear to be coming from a local service. Some other common things spoofed are MAC addresses and IP addresses.

DEAUTHENTICATION

Wireless deauthentication is when an attacker makes you deauthenticated with your network by sending *deauth packets* to your network router. Stopping this attack is nearly impossible, so the best thing to do is use a long patch cable. IEEE 802.11w addresses this issue by encrypting management frames.

BRUTE FORCE

A brute force attack is an attack in which the attacker repeatedly tries to guess your password in order to authenticate. The most common and effective use of this is a *dictionary attack*. A dictionary attack uses a pre-generated wordlist of common passphrases to gain access. This works very often on people who do not have secure (complex and lengthy) passwords.

More savvy users will require more advanced attacks. A basic brute force attack will try every possible combination to gain access. This can be extremely slow and often doesn't work online because many websites only allow a certain number of password attempts. A more successful method for brute forcing is brute forcing a password hash. If you can obtain the hashed password you can do the cracking offline.

VLAN HOPPING

Many organizations allow certain privileges to certain VLANs on a network. An attacker might use one of two methods to hop from one VLAN to another, gaining the privileges of the other VLAN.

The first method is *switch spoofing*, which takes advantage of automatic configuration in switches that allows you to pretend to be a switch, requiring no authentication. To protect against this, you should disable trunk negotiation.

The second method is *double tagging*, which is when an attacker puts two VLAN tags on a packet. The first switch that the packet contacts removes the first tag, and the second switch sees the second (fake) tag which it uses to forward the packet. To prevent this, you should not allow access to the native VLAN.

MAN-IN-THE-MIDDLE

A MITM attack is one in which the attacker sits between you and another device and views the traffic. It usually spoofs both machines, receiving device A packets as device B, viewing them, and then forwarding them to device B spoofed as device A.

EXPLOITS VS VULNERABILITIES

A vulnerability is a weakness. It's a flaw that *could* allow an attacker to access your network. For example, in a house: you may leave a window open or a door unlocked. Nobody has broken into your house, but the potential is there. In terms of a network, you may have a misconfigured network or bad password.

When somebody takes advantage of a vulnerability, they are *exploiting* the vulnerability. Exploits are built to take advantage of specific vulnerabilities. A *zero-day* attack is an attack that uses a vulnerability that the developer is not aware of.

NETWORK DEVICE HARDENING

To prevent attacks on your network, it is important to implement the following device hardening techniques into your organization's procedures.

CHANGING DEFAULT CREDENTIALS

When you add a new device to your network such as a router, it almost always has a default username and password. If you don't change these, attackers will have easy administrator access to your network.

AVOID COMMON PASSWORDS

When you create passwords, avoid very common or single word passwords. To create secure passwords, they should be a certain length and have special characters and numbers included.

UPGRADING FIRMWARE

Most network devices don't use typical desktop-oriented operating systems such as Windows, so upgrading network devices involves upgrading its firmware. Be sure to keep backups of your devices' configurations incase issues arise from updates.

PATCHING AND UPDATES

Common operating systems usually have some form of patch management. It's important to keep up-to-date on all patches and updates supplied to the devices on your network.

FILE HASHING

A hash is an irreversible string encoding method. These hashes can be used to check if the data you are accessing has changed by hashing the data and comparing it to the other hash.

DISABLING UNNECESSARY SERVICES

If a service is not in use, there is no point in leaving it running. Disabling it will prevent it from being used as an attack method against your network. Determining which services are unnecessary may require some trial and error.

USING SECURE PROTOCOLS

Be sure you are using only encrypted protocols for any data communication. Using HTTP over HTTPS for example can allow an attacker to view sensitive data in plain text. Use SSH over Telnet, SFTP over FTP, etc.

GENERATING NEW KEYS

Every encryption method uses some form of key to perform the encryption, be sure to change these when you install a device. These keys are often managed on servers. It's important to keep these keys protected, and change them frequently.

DISABLING UNUSED PORTS

If a port is not being used, disabling it will limit the access points for an attacker. For example, if your network does not need SSH, disabling port 22 will protect from an attacker using that port to connect to a device.

This also includes physical ports. If a port on a switch or router is not needed, it is good practice to put that port in an unused VLAN and disable the port.

MITIGATION TECHNIQUES: NETWORK

This section will detail the methods used to mitigate attacks by taking security actions related to the network.

DEVICE HARDENING

No device is secure with a default configuration, so be sure to go through the device hardening steps or a provided device hardening guide to secure your network devices.

CHANGE NATIVE VLAN

The native VLAN is used when trunking switches together. The native VLAN uses non-trunked frames (without the 802.1Q header). The default VLAN for the native VLAN is VLAN 1, which should be changed.

SWITCH PORT PROTECTION

SPANNING TREE: Spanning tree protocol designates certain ports as either a root port, designated port, or blocked port. This protocol prevents switch loops from occurring in your network. This protocol can even adapt to changes in the network connection. Spanning Tree should be enabled by default on most modern switches.

FLOOD GUARD: A flood guard will limit the number of MAC addresses that can be on an interface to prevent flooding. The interface will be disabled when that limit is reached.

BPDU GUARD: Bridge Protocol Data Unit (BPDU), sometimes called PortFast, it bypasses the listening and learning states of a switch when using spanning tree protocol.

ROOT GUARD: One switch in a network is designated as the root bridge; root guard prevents this root bridge from being changed.

DHCP SNOOPING: This will prevent rogue DHCP servers to be configured on your network, allowing you to choose trusted interfaces on your network and filter untrusted data out.

NETWORK SEGMENTATION

Segmenting a network can provide benefits to performance, security, and simplicity of your network. There are several ways of doing this.

DMZ: A DMZ switch adds additional security between two points, adding an entirely separate network for certain services.

VLAN: A VLAN segments a network by dividing its switch's ports into separate logical networks.

FILE INTEGRITY MONITORING

Some files should never change on a system. A FIM can check files on a system and see that nothing has changed when it was not supposed to (such as system files).

RESTRICTING ACCESS VIA ACLS

You can set up ACLs to limit access to certain devices. They can be configured to drop all traffic for non-authorized devices.

HONEYPOT / HONEYNET

A honeypot is a device that hosts a port or interface on your network and fakes a network to any incoming traffic. For example, you may leave port 8080 open on a device, and when an attacker tries to access this port, they proceed to access other devices on the network, however the network they are accessing doesn't actually exist and was set up beforehand to prevent the attacker from getting to the real network. The key is to set up proper alerts to let you know when an attacker has accessed your honeypot. You can then investigate their method of entry, block their access, and also capture / provide information to the proper authorities.

MITIGATION TECHNIQUES: POLICY

This section will detail methods of mitigating attacks using organization policy.

SIGNATURE MANAGEMENT

You should have policies in place dictating what happens when unwanted / malicious traffic is detected. It is common to group rules together and make decisions based on category.

PRIVILEGED USER ACCOUNT

A privileged user account has elevated access and can control almost everything. It's a good idea to take special care when securing this account using multi-factor authentication or other methods. Also, use a different login for an administrator account with less permissions.

ROLE SEPARATION

Role separation (or separation of duties) is the practice of separating employees into roles based on the functions they need to be able to perform on your network. You should only grant privileges to users that are necessary for them to perform their job. Role separation is the best defense against insider threats and you should have detailed policies in place such as AUPs.

PENETRATION TESTING

Penetration testing is one of the best ways to secure your network. It is the process of trying to hack your own network to discover vulnerabilities. You can either do this internally or bring in a third party to try and exploit your network's defenses.

TROUBLESHOOTING & TOOLS

TROUBLESHOOTING & TOOLS

Even the most seasoned administrators regularly encounter network issues that need to be resolved. After all, that is job security! This section will teach you about identifying and resolving common network problems.

A network troubleshooting methodology will be presented to ensure you are asking the right questions while troubleshooting a network problem. This methodology can be used on anything from simple home networks to complex networks powering global businesses.

No section on network troubleshooting would be complete without mentioning the tools that support it. Here we will cover industry-standard hardware and software tools that aid in monitoring and configuring a network.

Finally, we will describe a wide array of issues which can occur throughout the lifecycle of a network. This includes common issues in wired networks, wireless networks, and network services. Understanding how and why these problems occur is a key component of identifying and resolving future incidents within your environment.

METHODOLOGIES

It's very common for errors to occur when creating or configuring a network. When faced with these errors, it's helpful to go through the following methodologies.

1. IDENTIFY THE PROBLEM.

The first step to solving any problem is identifying what knowing what exactly the problem is. The following methods can be helpful for doing this:

- Gather information.
- Duplicate the problem, if possible.
- Ask the user about the problem and when it originated.
- Identify symptoms.
- Determine if anything has changed and if the technology in question ever functioned properly.
- Approach multiple problems one at a time.

2. ESTABLISH A THEORY OF PROBABLE CAUSE.

This should include:

- Questioning the obvious. The easiest solution is often the correct one, so start with the basics.
- Consider multiple approaches. Go through the OSI model top-to-bottom or bottom-to-top. Split coworkers up to look into different theories (divide and conquer).

3. TEST THE THEORY TO DETERMINE THE CAUSE.

For example, if you think the router is configured incorrectly, test your theory by sending something through the router.

- If the theory is correct, continue to determine the next steps for solving the problem.
- If the theory is incorrect, continue to theorize the cause of the problem and test.

4. ESTABLISH A PLAN TO RESOLVE THE PROBLEM & IDENTIFY POTENTIAL EFFECTS.

- Determine if your solution affects anything aside from the problem. Sometimes a solution can cause a new problem which is best to avoid.

5. IMPLEMENT THE SOLUTION.

- After creating a thought out plan, implement that solution to fix the issue.

6. VERIFY THE SYSTEM WORKS CORRECTLY.

- Test that the issue has been resolved.
- Test that other functionalities still work.
- Implement preventive measures if applicable.

7. DOCUMENT FINDINGS, ACTIONS, AND OUTCOMES.

- Record the issue, its cause, the solution, and the result of the solution.

TOOLS

One of the most important parts of implementing a system correctly is using the correct tools. This section goes over some common hardware and software tools that are important for setting up, configuring, and testing a network.

HARDWARE TOOLS

The following are used for configuring and testing the hardware involved in a network.

CRIMPER: Used to attach a connector to the end of a cable. You will first need to use wire strippers to expose the conductive part of the cable before crimping the connector on.

CABLE TESTER: Cable testers have a main role of determining if a cable is functioning properly. They can often tell you if the cable is straight-through or crossover as well as if it has any grounding issues.

PUNCHDOWN TOOLS: These are used to "punch" a wire down into an Insulated Displacement Connector (IDC).

OPTICAL TIME-DOMAIN REFLECTOMETER (OTDR): OTDRs are used to test fiber-optic cables. They can tell you the estimated length of the cable, the overall attenuation, and location faults such as breaks.

LIGHT METER: Simply tests if light is traveling correctly down a fiber.

TONE GENERATOR: These test simple copper wires by attaching to either side and emitting a tone when conduction occurs.

LOOPBACK ADAPTER: A device that loops an ethernet or fiber optic signal back to its sender. It is used to evaluate the integrity of the equipment or transmission path.

MULTIMETER: An electronic measuring instrument. These are commonly capable of measuring voltage, current, and resistance. They come in analog and digital form.

SPECTRUM ANALYZER: Measures the magnitude of an input signal versus the frequency. Its main use is to measure the power of the spectrum of known and unknown signals.

SOFTWARE TOOLS

Software tools are just as important as hardware tools. These are the most common software tools for testing and configuring a network.

PACKET SNIFFER: A program that looks inside every packet on a network segment and determines if there are any issues such as bottlenecks, retransmissions, or security breaches.

PORT SCANNER: A program used to identify open ports/services on a host. This information can be used to help determine the security posture of the host.

PROTOCOL ANALYZER: Works similarly to a packet sniffer in that it collects packets. It also analyzes the data and presents it in a human-readable way.

WI-FI ANALYZER: Used to sniff wireless networks. They can tell you the channels in use, the amount of clients, and bandwidth used, top talkers and more.

BANDWIDTH SPEED TESTER: Simply provides information about your internet connection such as bandwidth, upload speed, and download speed.

COMMAND LINE: A very important tool for performing network operations on a host machine. To see the usage of a command and its options you can use the command "man <command name>". Some commands include:

- **PING:** Tests a connection between hosts. When you *ping* a host, the program will tell you if it received a signal back and how long it took.
  ex. *C:\> ping 192.168.1.10*

- **TRACEROUTE (TRACERT ON WINDOWS):** Shows every router interface a TCP/IP packet passes through on its way to its destination.
  ex. *C:\> tracert www.website.com*

- **NSLOOKUP:** A Windows command that allows you to verify DNS resolutions to determine what IP address a host name resolves to.
  ex. *C:\> nslookup*
      > www.website.com

- **IPCONFIG:** Displays the basic routed protocol information of the host.
  ex. *C:\> ipconfig*

- **IFCONFIG:** The Unix alternative to ipconfig. Can also be used to change settings.
  ex. *$ ifconfig eth0*

- **IPTABLES:** This command is used to view and configure firewall settings on Unix based hosts. You can configure the firewall to accept or drop connections on particular ports.
  ex. *$ iptables -A INPUT -i eth0 -p tcp --dport 22 -m state --state NEW -j ACCEPT.*
  Creates a rule to make the firewall accept input through port 22.

- **NETSTAT:** This utility can be used to check the TCP/IP connections on your machine. It can also be used to view stats such as how many packets have been sent and received, errors, and so on.
  ex. *$ netstat*

- **TCPDUMP:** A common packet analyzer which allows you to view TCP/IP traffic.
  ex. *$ tcpdump host sundown*
  Shows traffic departing or arriving from sundown.

- **PATHPING:** Combines the functionality of ping and tracert. It provides details of the path between two hosts.
  ex. *C:\> pathping www.website.com*

- **NMAP:** Used to discover the nodes on a network. It then creates a "map" of the network.
  ex. *$ nmap www.website.com*

- **ROUTE:** Can be used to manipulate the routing table on a Windows Server.
  ex. *route print*
  Prints the current routes.

- **ARP:** A protocol in the TCP/IP suite which is used to determine MAC address to IP mappings. So the *arp* command is used to show and configure these mappings.
  ex. *C:\> arp*

- **DIG:** The Unix counterpart to nslookup. It allows you to query DNS for records or resolve host names.
  ex. *$ dig www.website.com*

CONNECTIVITY & PERFORMANCE ISSUES

When creating and configuring a network, there is a myriad of issues that can occur. Below are some of the most common issues that occur on both wired and wireless networks.

WIRED ISSUES

ATTENUATION: Attenuation / DB Loss / Distance Limitation occurs when the signal traveling over a wire degrades over a certain distance. Attenuation can affect copper wires at distances over 100 meters, at which point they will need to be amplified, repeated, or replaced with fiber.

LATENCY: This is the amount of time between when a signal is emitted and when it is received. If the latency is too high it can affect the efficiency or even effectiveness of a network. The best way to deal with high latency is to ensure your equipment such as routers are high quality.

JITTER: The fluctuation of latency over time. The cause of jitter is often the same cause of high latency, so it's important to ensure you have high quality equipment and cables, using a wired connection over wireless when possible. This can be extremely detrimental in time sensitive communications such as live streaming video and VoIP.

CROSSTALK: This can occur when signal bleeds between two adjacent wires carrying a current. This is prevented by twisting the wire pairs together, putting them at a 90-degree angle to each other. The tighter the wires are twisted, the more of a difference it will make.

EMI & RFI: Electromagnetic Interference and Radio Frequency Interference occur when signals interfere with the normal operation of electronic circuits. Cell phones / TVs can cause this. The best way to prevent this is shielded network cables such as Shielded Twisted Pair (STP).

OPEN / SHORT: This occurs when the intended path for a cable is misdirected, or *shorted*. This is usually caused by a physical issue with the cable but sometimes when a network is connected incorrectly. Use circuit-testing tools to test your wires and replace any that do not work properly.

INCORRECT PIN-OUT: Occurs when the twisted-pairs of a cable are not connected to the proper pins. This can sometimes be hard to detect, so keep this in mind when debugging your network.

INCORRECT CABLE TYPE: This issue is usually obvious. It's important to check that you're using the correct cable for the specific function you're trying to perform, i.e., a Cat 5 cable for Internet.

BAD PORT: A bad port will often result in complete loss of connection. Similar symptoms occur from a bad cable and bad port, so test the cable first.

TRANSCEIVER MISMATCH: This is an issue when fiber-optic transceivers are using a different wavelength or if one transceiver has gone bad.

TX/RX REVERSE: When connecting a machine to a switch, the PC uses pins 1 and 2 to transmit and 3 and 4 to receive. This means the switch must use pins 1 and 2 to receive and 3 and 4 to transmit. Be sure to verify this.

DUPLEX/SPEED MISMATCH: This occurs when two connected devices are set with different duplex modes (one in half-duplex and the other in full-duplex). This will cause the connection to operate inefficiently.

BOTTLENECKS: This issue occurs when a part of the network is limiting throughput. If a network device is operating below its intended potential, check its path throughout the network for anything that would limit its throughput.

VLAN MISMATCH: This occurs when a VLAN is misconfigured. For example, ethernet port 1 is configured to the wrong VLAN, making the host connected to it part of the wrong network.

OTHER ISSUES:
- Damaged cables
- Bent pins

NOTE: Look at network connection LED status indicators to verify a connection is occurring. This is often found near the connector.

WIRELESS ISSUES

REFLECTION: Occurs when the entire signal does not reach its destination and is instead reflected back or away. This can be caused by certain materials such as metal.

REFRACTION: Occurs when the signal passes through a material that bends the electromagnetic waves (such as glass or water).

ABSORPTION: Some materials can absorb the signal such as wood or concrete and have a significant impact on the signal.

INCORRECT ANTENNA TYPE: The type of antenna you are using is not applicable for your specific network (i.e., using a unidirectional broadcast rather than an omnidirectional one).

INCORRECT ANTENNA PLACEMENT: When your antenna is located in an area where the signal can be easily interfered with. It's important to place your antenna in a central location out of the way from obstructions.

CHANNEL OVERLAP: When multiple APs use the same channel within a small space, you will often get channel overlap which can cause a lot of interference.

OVERCAPACITY: This occurs when too many devices are connected on a single AP. This issue can be resolved either by limited the number of devices, or creating additional access points.

DISTANCE LIMITATIONS: When a device is outside of the range of an AP, this is called a distance limitation. It's important to keep range requirements in mind when building your network.

FREQUENCY MISMATCH: An AP can often be configured to use different frequencies. Ensure the frequency matches the one that devices will try to connect with to prevent a frequency mismatch.

SIGNAL-TO-NOISE RATIO: This is a measurement of the amount of signal compared to how much interference there is. A high signal-to-noise ratio means clearer signal.

OTHER ISSUES:

- **POWER:** The signal strength is not great enough for the user, which can be solved by moving the AP closer to them or getting a stronger antenna.

- **WRONG SSID:** The user is trying to connect to the wrong network.

- **SECURITY TYPE MISMATCH:** The user is trying to authenticate incorrectly, i.e. using WEP instead of WPA2.

- **WRONG PASSPHRASE:** The user is entering the wrong password to authenticate.

SERVICE ISSUES

Aside from wired and wireless connectivity issues occurring, there is also the possibility that the services on your network such as DNS and DHCP will run into issues. Below are the common service issues you will run into.

NAMES NOT RESOLVING

DNS addresses are usually configured automatically by a DHCP server, but sometimes these addresses are configured statically. If a hostname is configured incorrectly it can cause applications that rely on them to mess up.

INCORRECT GATEWAY

Every device needs a gateway, or *default gateway*, to send traffic outside of the local network. A device with a misconfigured default gateway address can cause it to be unable to communicate with the network correctly.

INCORRECT NETMASK

A device uses a subnet mask to determine which part of the IP address is the host address and which part is the network address. This means an incorrect subnet mask is as bad as an incorrect IP address, making a host unable to communicate with another host.

DUPLICATE IP ADDRESS

Normally, computers get their IP address from a DHCP server on the network, but it's common in smaller networks for IP addresses to be assigned statically. This introduces the potential for duplicate IP addresses, i.e., assigning an IP address to a computer already in use on the network.

EXPIRED IP ADDRESS

When an IP address is assigned from a DHCP server, it's given a lease time, after which the IP address must be renewed. If the device is unable to renew from the DHCP server, it can cause the IP address to eventually expire.

ROGUE DHCP SERVER

This is a server performing DHCP functions that is not under the control of the administrator. It can be caused by an unaware user or an attacker in an attempt to perform a Man in the Middle (MITM) attack. Use an intrusion detection system (IDS) to prevent this issue.

UNTRUSTED SSL CERTIFICATE

When accessing a resource such as a website, it's possible to be given a security warning if the resource you are accessing is not signed by a trusted source. This is usually an issue with the resource itself, if you are the administrator be sure that the SSL certificate is valid.

INCORRECT TIME

Problems arise when the system time of a device is not in sync with that of the network. It's important to use NTP to avoid this issue.

EXHAUSTED DHCP SCOPE

DHCP servers are often configured to give out a certain pool of IP addresses, and as more devices are added to a network, those IP addresses can be used up. Potential solutions include allocating more IP addresses to the DHCP server or editing the subnet mask to create more IP addresses.

BLOCKED TCP/UDP PORTS

This issue is caused when a device is trying to access another through a certain port which is blocked. For example, trying to use SSH to connect to a remote device while port 22 is blocked.

INCORRECT HOST-BASED FIREWALL SETTINGS

Most devices have their own firewall which can prevent incoming or outgoing connections from the device. Ensure that all firewalls on the network are open to the necessary connections.

INCORRECT ACL SETTINGS

Access Control List (ACL) defines the allowed connections by a firewall; a bad configuration can prevent important connections in a network or allow bad connections.

UNRESPONSIVE SERVICE

Sometimes a service doesn't work not because of a misconfigured network, but because it has become unresponsive. In this case you can often restart the service, but be careful to think of what will happen when you do.

HARDWARE FAILURE

A hardware failure is another potential cause of a service not working. This should be one of the first things you check for when debugging your service.

NOTES

ACRONYMS SPELLED OUT

AAA	Authentication Authorization and Accounting
AAAA	Authentication, Authorization, Accounting and Auditing
ACL	Access Control List
ADSL	Asymmetric Digital Subscriber Line
AES	Advanced Encryption Standard
AH	Authentication Header
AP	Access Point
APC	Angle Polished Connector
APIPA	Automatic Private Internet Protocol Addressing
APT	Advanced Persistent Tool
ARIN	American Registry for Internet Numbers
ARP	Address Resolution Protocol
AS	Autonomous System
ASCII	American Standard Code for Information Exchange
ASIC	Application Specific Integrated Circuit
ASP	Application Service Provider
ATM	Asynchronous Transfer Mode
AUP	Acceptable Use Policy
Auto-MDX	Automatic Medium-Dependent Interface Crossover
BCP	Business Continuity Plan
BERT	Bit-Error Rate Test
BGP	Border Gateway Protocol
BLE	Bluetooth Low Energy

BNC	British Naval Connector/Bayonet Niell-Concelman
BootP	Boot Protocol/Bootstrap Protocol
BPDU	Bridge Protocol Data Unit
BRI	Basic Rate Interface
BSSID	Basic Service Set Identifier
BYOD	Bring Your Own Device
CaaS	Communication as a Service
CAM	Content Addressable Memory
CAN	Campus Area Network
CARP	Common Address Redundancy Protocol
CASB	Cloud Access Security Broker
CAT	Category
CCMP	Counter-mode Cipher Block Chaining Message Authentication Code Protocol
CCTV	Closed Circuit TV
CDMA	Code Division Multiple Access
CSMA/CD	Carrier Sense Multiple Access/Collision Detection
CHAP	Challenge Handshake Authentication Protocol
CIDR	Classless Inter-Domain Routing
CIFS	Common Internet File System
CNAME	Canonical Name
CoS	Class of Service
CPU	Central Processing Unit
CRAM-MD5	Challenge-Response Authentication Mechanism-Message Digest 5

CRC	Cyclic Redundancy Checking
CSMA/CA	Carrier Sense Multiple Access/Collision Avoidance
CSU	Channel Service Unit
CVE	Common Vulnerabilities and Exposures
CVW	Collaborative Virtual Workspace
CWDM	Coarse Wave Division Multiplexing
Daas	Desktop as a Service
dB	Decibel
DCS	Distributed Computer System
DDoS	Distributed Denial of Service
DHCP	Dynamic Host Configuration Protocol
DLC	Data Link Control
DLP	Data Loss Prevention
DLR	Device Level Ring
DMVPN	Dynamic Multipoint Virtual Private Network
DMZ	Demilitarized Zone
DNAT	Destination Network Address Translation
DNS	Domain Name Service/Domain Name Server/Domain Name System
DOCSIS	Data-Over-Cable Service Interface Specification
DoS	Denial of Service
DPI	Deep Packet Inspection
DR	Designated Router
DSCP	Differentiated Services Code Point

DSL	Digital Subscriber Line
DSSS	Direct Sequence Spread Spectrum
DSU	Data Service Unit
DTLS	Datagram Transport Layer Security
DWDM	Dense Wavelength Division Multiplexing
E1	E-Carrier Level 1
EAP	Extensible Authentication Protocol
EBCDIC	Extended Binary Coded Decimal Interchange Code
EDNS	Extension Mechanisms for DNS
EGP	Exterior Gateway Protocol
EMI	Electromagnetic Interference
ESD	Electrostatic Discharge
ESP	Encapsulated Security Payload
ESSID	Extended Service Set Identifier
EUI	Extended Unique Identifier
FC	Fibre Channel
FCoE	Fibre Channel over Ethernet
FCS	Frame Check Sequence
FDM	Frequency Division Multiplexing
FHSS	Frequency Hopping Spread Spectrum
FM	Frequency Modulation
FQDN	Fully Qualified Domain Name
FTP	File Transfer Protocol

FTPS	File Transfer Protocol Security
GBIC	Gigabit Interface Converter
Gbps	Gigabits per second
GLBP	Gateway Load Balancing Protocol
GPG	GNU Privacy Guard
GRE	Generic Routing Encapsulation
GSM	Global System for Mobile Communications
HA	High Availability
HDLC	High-Level Data Link Control
HDMI	High-Definition Multimedia Interface
HIDS	Host Intrusion Detection System
HIPS	Host Intrusion Prevention System
HSPA	High-Speed Packet Access
HSRP	Hot Standby Router Protocol
HT	High Throughput
HTTP	Hypertext Transfer Protocol
HTTPS	Hypertext Transfer Protocol Secure
HVAC	Heating, Ventilation and Air Conditioning
Hz	Hertz
IaaS	Infrastructure as a Service
IANA	Internet Assigned Numbers Authority
ICA	Independent Computer Architecture
ICANN	Internet Corporation for Assigned Names and Numbers

ICMP	Internet Control Message Protocol
ICS	Internet Connection Sharing/Industrial Control System
IDF	Intermediate Distribution Frame
IDS	Intrusion Detection System
IEEE	Institute of Electrical and Electronics Engineers
IGMP	Internet Group Message Protocol
IGP	Interior Gateway Protocol
IGRP	Interior Gateway Routing Protocol
IKE	Internet Key Exchange
IMAP4	Internet Message Access Protocol version 4
InterNIC	Internet Network Information Center
IoT	Internet of Things
IP	Internet Protocol
IPAM	IP Address Management
IPS	Intrusion Prevention System
IPSec	Internet Protocol Security
IPv4	Internet Protocol version 4
IPv6	Internet Protocol version 6
ISAKMP	Internet Security Association and Key Management Protocol
ISDN	Integrated Services Digital Network
IS-IS	Intermediate System to Intermediate System
ISP	Internet Service Provider
IT	Information Technology

ITS	Intelligent Transportation System
IV	Initialization Vector
Kbps	Kilobits per second
KVM	Keyboard Video Mouse
L2TP	Layer 2 Tunneling Protocol
LACP	Link Aggregation Control Protocol
LAN	Local Area Network
LC	Local Connector
LDAP	Lightweight Directory Access Protocol
LEC	Local Exchange Carrier
LED	Light Emitting Diode
LLC	Logical Link Control
LLDP	Link Layer Discovery Protocol
LSA	Link State Advertisements
LTE	Long Term Evolution
LWAPP	Light Weight Access Point Protocol
MaaS	Mobility as a Service
MAC	Media Access Control/Medium Access Control
MAN	Metropolitan Area Network
Mbps	Megabits per second
MBps	Megabytes per second
MDF	Main Distribution Frame
MDI	Media Dependent Interface

MDIX	Media Dependent Interface Crossover
MFA	Multifactor Authentication
MGCP	Media Gateway Control Protocol
MIB	Management Information Base
MIMO	Multiple Input, Multiple Output
MLA	Master License Agreement/Multilateral Agreement
MMF	Multimode Fiber
MOA	Memorandum of Agreement
MOU	Memorandum of Understanding
MPLS	Multiprotocol Label Switching
MS-CHAP	Microsoft Challenge Handshake Authentication Protocol
MSA	Master Service Agreement
MSDS	Material Safety Data Sheet
MT-RJ	Mechanical Transfer-Registered Jack
MTU	Maximum Transmission Unit
MTTR	Mean Time To Recovery
MTBF	Mean Time Between Failures
MU-MIMO	Multiuser Multiple Input, Multiple Output
MX	Mail Exchanger
NAC	Network Access Control
NAS	Network Attached Storage
NAT	Network Address Translation
NCP	Network Control Protocol

NDR	Non-Delivery Receipt
NetBEUI	Network Basic Input/Output Extended User Interface
NetBIOS	Network Basic Input/Output System
NFC	Near Field Communication
NFS	Network File Service
NGFW	Next-Generation Firewall
NIC	Network Interface Card
NIDS	Network Intrusion Detection System
NIPS	Network Intrusion Prevention System
NIU	Network Interface Unit
nm	Nanometer
NNTP	Network News Transport Protocol
NTP	Network Time Protocol
OCSP	Online Certificate Status Protocol
OCx	Optical Carrier
OID	Object Identifier
OOB	Out of Band
OS	Operating System
OSI	Open Systems Interconnect
OSPF	Open Shortest Path First
OTDR	Optical Time Domain Reflectometer
OUI	Organizationally Unique Identifier
PaaS	Platform as a Service

PAN	Personal Area Network
PAP	Password Authentication Protocol
PAT	Port Address Translation
PC	Personal Computer
PCM	Phase-Change Memory
PDoS	Permanent Denial of Service
PDU	Protocol Data Unit
PGP	Pretty Good Privacy
PKI	Public Key Infrastructure
PoE	Power over Ethernet
POP	Post Office Protocol
POP3	Post Office Protocol version 3
POTS	Plain Old Telephone Service
PPP	Point-to-Point Protocol
PPPoE	Point-to-Point Protocol over Ethernet
PPTP	Point-to-Point Tunneling Protocol
PRI	Primary Rate Interface
PSK	Pre-Shared Key
PSTN	Public Switched Telephone Network
PTP	Point-to-Point
PTR	Pointer
PUA	Privileged User Agreement
PVC	Permanent Virtual Circuit

QoS	Quality of Service
QSFP	Quad Small Form-Factor Pluggable
RADIUS	Remote Authentication Dial-In User Service
RARP	Reverse Address Resolution Protocol
RAS	Remote Access Service
RDP	Remote Desktop Protocol
RF	Radio Frequency
RFI	Radio Frequency Interference
RFP	Request for Proposal
RG	Radio Guide
RIP	Routing Internet Protocol
RJ	Registered Jack
RPO	Recovery Point Objective
RSA	Rivest, Shamir, Adelman
RSH	Remote Shell
RSTP	Rapid Spanning Tree Protocol
RTO	Recovery Time Objective
RTP	Real-Time Protocol
RTSP	Real-Time Streaming Protocol
RTT	Round Trip Time or Real Transfer Time
SA	Security Association
SaaS	Software as a Service
SAN	Storage Area Network

SC	Standard Connector/Subscriber Connector
SCADA	Supervisory Control and Data Acquisition
SCP	Secure Copy Protocol
SCSI	Small Computer System Interface
SDLC	Software Development Life Cycle
SDN	Software Defined Network
SDP	Session Description Protocol
SDSL	Symmetrical Digital Subscriber Line
SECaaS	Security as a Service
SFP	Small Form-factor Pluggable
SFTP	Secure File Transfer Protocol
SGCP	Simple Gateway Control Protocol
SHA	Secure Hash Algorithm
SIEM	Security Information and Event Management
SIP	Session Initiation Protocol
SLA	Service Level Agreement
SLAAC	Stateless Address Auto Configuration
SLIP	Serial Line Internet Protocol
SMB	Server Message Block
SMF	Single-Mode Fiber
SMS	Short Message Service
SMTP	Simple Mail Transfer Protocol
SNAT	Static Network Address Translation/Source Network Address Translation

SNMP	Simple Network Management Protocol	
SNR	Signal-to-Noise Ratio	
SNTP	Simple Network Time Protocol	
SOA	Start of Authority	
SOHO	Small Office Home Office	
SONET	Synchronous Optical Network	
SOP	Standard Operating Procedure	
SOW	Statement of Work	
SPB	Shortest Path Bridging	
SPI	Stateful Packet Inspection	
SPS	Standby Power Supply	
SSH	Secure Shell	
SSID	Service Set Identifier	
SSL	Secure Sockets Layer	
SSO	Single Sign-on	
ST	Straight Tip (or) Snap Twist	
STP	Spanning Tree Protocol/Shielded Twisted Pair	
SVC	Switched Virtual Circuit	
SYSLOG	System Log	
T1	Terrestrial Carrier Level 1	
TA	Terminal Adaptor	
TACACS	Terminal Access Control Access Control System	
TACACS+	Terminal Access Control Access Control System+	

TCP	Transmission Control Protocol
TCP/IP	Transmission Control Protocol/Internet Protocol
TDM	Time Division Multiplexing
TDR	Time Domain Reflectometer
Telco	Telecommunications Company
TFTP	Trivial File Transfer Protocol
TIA/EIA	Telecommunication Industries Association/Electronic Industries Alliance
TKIP	Temporal Key Integrity Protocol
TLS	Transport Layer Security
TMS	Transportation Management System
TOS	Type of Service
TPM	Trusted Platform Module
TTL	Time to Live
TTLS	Tunneled Transport Layer Security
UC	Unified Communications
UDP	User Datagram Protocol
UNC	Universal Naming Convention
UPC	Ultra Polished Connector
UPS	Uninterruptible Power Supply
URL	Uniform Resource Locator
USB	Universal Serial Bus
UTM	Unified Threat Management
UTP	Unshielded Twisted Pair

VDSL	Variable Digital Subscriber Line
VLAN	Virtual Local Area Network
VLSM	Variable Length Subnet Mask
VNC	Virtual Network Connection
VoIP	Voice over IP
VPN	Virtual Private Network
VRF	Virtual Routing Forwarding
VRRP	Virtual Router Redundancy Protocol
VTC	Video Teleconference
VTP	VLAN Trunk Protocol
WAF	Web Application Firewall
WAN	Wide Area Network

Made in the USA
Columbia, SC
04 January 2022

53501519R00088